SELECTED POEMS

Thomas Lux was born in Northampton, Massachusetts, in December 1946, to working-class parents. He was raised on a dairy farm. He studied at Emerson College, Boston, and later, briefly, at the University of Iowa. He taught for 27 years at Sarah Lawrence College, has done spells of teaching at many other universities across the States, and is now Bourne Professor of Poetry and director of Poetry@Tech at the Georgia Institute of Technology in Atlanta.

He has published twelve collections of poetry. His "switchover" collection was *Half Promised Land* in 1986, which marked a sea change in his work. *Split Horizon* in 1994 won him the Kingsley-Tufts Award, making it possible for him to devote much more time and energy to his poetry at a crucial stage in the evolution of his work. His later books include *New and Selected Poems 1975-1995*, published in 1997, which shows the poet before and after his "recovery" from Surrealism, and was followed by *The Street of Clocks* (2001), *The Cradle Place* (2004), *God Particles* (2008) and *Child Made of Sand* (2012). He has published two books of poetry in Britain, *The Street of Clocks* – from Arc in 2001 – and now his *Selected Poems* (2014) from Bloodaxe.

THOMAS LUX

SELECTED
POEMS
1982-2012

BLOODAXE BOOKS

ISBN: 978 1 78037 115 3

First published 2014 by
Bloodaxe Books Ltd,
Eastburn,
South Park,
Hexham,
Northumberland NE46 1BS.

www.bloodaxebooks.com
For further information about Bloodaxe titles
please visit our website or write to
the above address for a catalogue.

Supported using public funding by
ARTS COUNCIL
ENGLAND

ACKNOWLEDGEMENTS

The poems in this edition are selected from the following books published in
the US by Houghton Mifflin, by permission of the author and publisher:
Half Promised Land (1986), *The Drowned River* (1990), *Split Horizon* (1994),
New and Selected Poems 1975-1995 (1997), *The Street of Clocks* (2001),
The Cradle Place (2004), *God Particles* (2008) and *Child Made of Sand* (2012).

Cover design: Neil Astley & Pamela Robertson-Pearce.

Printed in Great Britain by Bell & Bain Limited, Glasgow, Scotland, on
acid-free paper sourced from mills with FSC chain of custody certification.

...but in what is
ours, here, let
    justice be primary
when we sing,
    my dear.
                HAYDEN CARRUTH

to the most remote cell in the big toe.
                SHERWIN B. NULAND

The general was busy with the ant farm
    in his head.
                CHARLES SIMIC

CONTENTS

from NEW AND SELECTED POEMS (1997)

from THE STREET OF CLOCKS (2001)

from **CHILD MADE OF SAND** (2012)

FROM

Half Promised Land

(1986)

The Milkman and His Son

(for my father)

For a year he'd collect
the milk bottles – those cracked, chipped,
or with the label's blue
scene of a farm

fading. In winter
they'd load the boxes on a sled
and drag them to the dump

which was lovely then: a white sheet
drawn up, like a joke, over
the face of a sleeper.
As they lob the bottles in

the son begs a trick
and the milkman obliges: tossing
one bottle in a high arc,
he shatters it in midair

with another. One thousand astonished
splints of glass
falling.... Again
and again, and damned
if that milkman,
that easy slinger
on the dump's edge (as the drifted
junk tips its hats

of snow), damned if he didn't
hit almost half! Not bad.
Along with gentleness,

and the sane bewilderment
of understanding nothing cruel,
it was a thing he did best.

The Thirst of Turtles

How parched, how marrow-dust dry
they must get on their long surface and undersea
journeys – huge stuffed husks,
imperturbable swimmers grazing
jellyfish abutting the bruised
waters' pasture. How thirsty
a sixty-day swim, how graceful
the winching back to one unforgotten
shore. *Plub, plub*, sleepless
the hull's inner workings, their tails
motorless rudderings; deep,
deep their thirst and need. One hundred,
one hundred and twenty: how long they live
in their thirst, propelling
the great bloody steaks of their bodies,
dreaming, anticipating alert,
single-purposed oblivions: sweet
sweet turtle-sex – which excites
the lonely watches of sailors – sometimes days
joined in wave-riding rapture on the surface
of the depths. And still more thirsty
afterward, how alone later (currents
having taken) – righted, relentless,
back on course, collision, with centuries,
with a shore: solitary, speechless,
utterly buoyant, as unethereal
as cabbage. How thirsty these
both wise and clumsy, like us, feeding
in ever-widening or diminishing circles,
outward and inward, dropping
great oily tears, killing themselves
to beat a big hole in dirt,
burying something, then retreating
heavily on their own tracks, like rails,
reaching forward to the sea.

At the Far End of a Long Wharf

At the far end of a long wharf
a deaf child, while fishing, hauls in
a large eel and – not
because it is ugly – she bashes its brains
out of eeldom on the hot
planks – *whamp, whamp, whamp*, a sound
she does not hear. It's the distance
and the heat that abstracts
the image for me. She also does not hear,
nor do I, the splash the eel makes
when she tosses it in her bucket,
nor do we hear the new bait
pierced by the clean hook, nor
its lowering into the water again.
Nobody could. I watch her
all afternoon until, catching nothing
else, she walks the wharf toward
me, her cousin, thinking
with a thousand fingers. Pointing
at our boat she tells me
to drag it to the water. She wants me to row
her out to the deep lanes of fish.
Poetry is a menial task.

Tarantulas on the Lifebuoy

For some semitropical reason
when the rains fall
relentlessly they fall

into swimming pools, these otherwise
bright and scary
arachnids. They can swim
a little, but not for long

and they can't climb the ladder out.
They usually drown – but
if you want their favor,
if you believe there is justice,
a reward for not loving

the death of ugly
and even dangerous (the eel, hog snake,
rats) creatures, if

you believe these things, then
you would leave a lifebuoy
or two in your swimming pool at night.

And in the morning
you would haul ashore
the huddled, hairy survivors

and escort them
back to the bush, and know,
be assured that at least these saved,
as individuals, would not turn up

again someday
in your hat, drawer,
or the tangled underworld

of your socks, and that even –
when your belief in justice
merges with your belief in dreams –
they may tell the others

in a sign language
four times as subtle
and complicated as man's

that you are good,
that you love them,
that you would save them again.

The Night So Bright a Squirrel Reads

The night so bright a squirrel reads
a novel on his branch
without clicking on his lamp.
You know you're in a forest – the stars,
the moon blaring
off the white birch.... You could walk
out with your wife
into the forest, toward the fields beyond,
you could walk apart from her,
and still see her. It's so bright
you need not talk nor fear
that particular sticky abrasion you get
by walking into pine trees. You find
a lucidity in this darkness.
Your wife is here – three or four
trees away – you recognise her profile,
and you do not think she is anyone else,
here with you, a hundred
or so yards now from a field where,
in an hour or so, you might see
dawn's first deer browsing, or an owl,
soaring home after the shift he loves,
a fat sack of field mice under his wing.

It Must Be the Monk in Me

It must be the monk in me,
or the teenage girl. That's why I'm always off
somewhere in my mind with something
stupid (like a monk) or spiritual
(like a teenage girl). Sometimes, there's vision,
by reason of faith, in glimpses, or else,
and more often, a lovely blank, a hunger
like Moses' hunger when with his fingernails
he scraped the boulders of their meager lichen
and then fiercely sucking them.... It's a way
of living on the earth – to be away
from it part of the time. They say
it begins in childhood: your dog
gets runned over, your father
puts a knife to your mother's throat....
But those things only make you crazy
and don't account for scanning,
or actually mapping, a galaxy inside. I believe
it happens *before* birth, and has to do,
naturally, with Mom. Not with what she eats,
or does, or even thinks – but with what she *doesn't*
think, or want to: the knot of you growing larger
and, therefore, growing away.

The Dark Comes on in Blocks, in Cubes

The dark comes on in blocks, in cubes,
in cubics of black measured
perfectly, perfectly
filled. It's subtle and it's not,
depending on your point of view.
You can measure it best in a forest,
or in a grassy lowland, or in any place
where your lamp is the only lamp and you can turn it off.
To describe it the usual adjectives
of the gray/black genre will not do. It's not light,
nor is it the absence of light, but
oh, it's sweet, sweet like ink
dropped in sugar, necessary and invisible
like drafts of oxygen. Absolutely,
in squares, in its containers of space,
the darkness arrives – as daily
as bread, as sad as a haymow
going over and over a stubble field,
as routine as guards
climbing to gun towers
along penitentiary walls, clicking
on their searchlights
against it.

Wife Hits Moose

Sometime around dusk moose lifts
his heavy, primordial jaw, dripping, from pondwater
and, without psychic struggle,
decides the day, for him, is done: time
to go somewhere else. Meanwhile, wife
drives one of those roads that cut straight north,
a highway dividing the forests

not yet fat enough for the paper companies.
This time of year full dark falls
about eight o'clock – pineforest and blacktop
blend. Moose reaches road, fails
to look both ways, steps
deliberately, ponderously.... Wife
hits moose, hard,

at a slight angle (brakes slammed, car
spinning) and moose rolls over hood, antlers –
as if diamond-tipped – scratch windshield, car
damaged: rib-of-moose imprint
on fender, hoof shatters headlight.
Annoyed moose lands on feet and walks away.
Wife is shaken, unhurt, amazed.

– Does moose believe in a Supreme Intelligence?
Speaker does not know.
– Does wife believe in a Supreme Intelligence?
Speaker assumes as much: spiritual intimacies
being between the spirit and the human.
– Does speaker believe in a Supreme Intelligence?
Yes. Thank You.

The Swimming Pool

All around the apt. swimming pool
the boys stare at the girls
and the girls look everywhere but the opposite
or down or up. It is
as it was a thousand years ago: the fat
boy has it hardest, he
takes the sneers,
prefers the winter so he can wear
his heavy pants and sweater.
Today, he's here with the others.
Better they are cruel to him in his presence
than out. Of the five here now (three boys,
two girls) one is fat, three cruel,
and one, a girl, wavers to the side,
all the world tearing at her.
As yet she has no breasts
(her friend does) and were it not
for the forlorn fat boy whom she joins
in taunting, she could not bear her terror,
which is the terror
of being him. Does it make her happy
that she has no need, right now, of ingratiation,
of acting fool to salve
her loneliness? She doesn't seem
so happy. She is like
the lower middle class, that fatal group
handed crumbs so they can drop a few
down lower, to the poor, so they won't kill
the rich. All around
the apt. swimming pool
there is what's everywhere: forsakenness
and fear, a disdain for those beneath us
rather than a rage
against the ones above: the exploiters,
the oblivious and unabashedly cruel.

The Drowned River

(1990)

Backyard Swingset

Splayed, swayback, cheap pipe
playground: a swing, a slide, some rings
maybe – we love our babies,
and a tire hanging from a branch
won't do. For one summer
it shines – red, the chains of silver,
and beside it the blue plastic pool.
First winter out it goes to rust.
I love America's backyards,
seen from highways, or when
you're lost and looking

hard at houses, numbers.
The above, plus a washed-out willow,
starveling hedge, tool shed
a dozen times dented,
and a greasy streak
against the garage where a barbecue
went berserk. A Chevy engine block
never hauled away
or the classic Olds on chocks....
Beneath the blue-gray humps of snow: pieces
of a summer, a past

Mom said to pick up,
but they weren't.
Now, nobody's home, all across America
nobody's home now.
Brother or sister is, in fact, on Guam,
or working nightshift at the box factory,
or one is married and at this moment
wiping milk rings from a kitchen table.
And Mom, Mom is gone,
and the ash on Father's cigarette grows so long
it begins to chasm and bend.

Old Man Shoveling Snow

Bend your back to it, sir: for it will snow all night.
How gently they sink – white spiders,
multi-bladed bleak things,
these first, into the near mirror
of your shovel's surface. It snows,
lightly – wide columns
of black between each flake –

but it will snow all night, and thicker.
So you start now and scrape
your driveway of its first half inch.
Every hour you will plow
it down and up again.
It's not a grave
you dig, nor a path to school,

nor is there a dot of philosophy
in this work: you clear it as it falls
so as not to lift the heavy load at dawn.
The lanes behind you whiten,
imperceptibly hiss, and several –
smoke-roses, epaulets – bite
your back, your closed shoulders.

So soft, stubborn, it falls, parting
the streetlamp's light
harder, larger, and the whole cold neighborhood
bandaged. On the corner
the salt and sand box,
the mailbox (such white
on blue!) could be art

but aren't. You should move
a little faster now behind
the shovel – push once your twenty feet
of drive and it fills.
Soon it will take two.
Bend your back to it, sir: for it
will snow all night.

Cellar Stairs

It's rickety down to the dark.
Old skates, long-bladed, hang by leather laces
on your left and want to slash your throat,
but they can't, they can't, being only skates.
On a shelf above, tools: shears,
three-pronged weed hacker, ice pick,
poison – rats and bugs – and on the landing,
halfway down, a keg of roofing nails
you don't want to fall face first into,

no, you don't. To your right,
a fuse box with its side-switch – a slot machine,
on a good day, or the one the warden pulls,
on a bad. Against the wall,
on nearly every stair, one boot, no two
together, no pair, as if the dead
went off, short-legged or long, to where they go,
which is down these steps,
at the bottom of which is a swollen,

humming, huge white freezer
big enough for many bodies –
of children, at least. And this
is where you're sent each night
for the frozen bag of beans
or peas or broccoli
that lies beside the slab
of meat you'll eat for dinner,
each countless childhood meal your last.

So You Put the Dog to Sleep

I have no dog, but it must be
Somewhere there's one belongs to me.

JOHN KENDRICK BANGS

You love your dog and carve his steaks
(marbled, tender, aged) in the shape of hearts.
You let him on your lap at will

and call him by a lover's name: *Liebchen*,
pooch-o-mine, lamby, honey-tart,
and you fill your voice with tenderness, woo.

He loves you too, that's his only job,
it's how he pays his room and board.
Behind his devotion, though, his dopey looks,

might be a beast who wants your house,
your wife; who in fact loathes you, his lord.
His jaws snapping while asleep means dreams

of eating your face: nose, lips, eyebrows, ears...
But soon your dog gets old, his legs
go bad, he's nearly blind, you puree his meat

and feed him with a spoon. It's hard to say
who hates whom the most. He will not beg.
So you put the dog to sleep. Bad dog.

Traveling Exhibit of Torture Instruments

What man has done to woman and man
and the tools he built to do it with
is pure genius in its pain. A chair of nails
would not do without a headrest of spikes
and wrist straps pierced with pins.
The Head Crusher, for example – 'Experts disagree
about this piece: is it 17th or 18th century?'
This historical hatband contracts and contracts,
by screw, and was wrought by hand.
These skills, this craft, get passed along.
Take *The Red Hot Pincers and Tongs*.
They were 'addressed mostly to noses, fingers, toes.
Tubular pincers, like the splendid crocodile
shown here, served to rip off...' I have been in pain
at museums, openings, but not
like this: *The Heretic's Fork* – 'Placed
as it is, allows the victim only to murmur: I recant.'
In all the pictures
the men and women chosen do not
appear in pain: sawed lengthwise,
wrecked on a rack or wheel, they do not
look in pain. And the torturers
(the business always official)
seem uninterested, often flipping
pages of a book – one of laws, of God.
It seems most times men did this or that,
so terrible to him or her,
it was because God willed it so.
Or, at least, they thought He did.

Walt Whitman's Brain Dropped on Laboratory Floor

At his request, after death, his brain was removed
for science, phrenology, to study, and
as the mortuary assistant carried it (I suppose
in a jar but I hope cupped
in his hands) across the lab's stone floor, he dropped it.

You could ask a forensic pathologist
what that might look like. He willed his brain,
as I said, for study – its bumps and grooves,
analysed, allowing a deeper grasp
of human nature, potential (so phrenology believed),
and this kind of intense look, as opposed to mere fingering

of the skull's outer ridges, valleys, would afford
particular insight. So Walt believed.
He had already scored high (between a 6 and a 7) for Ego.
And as if we couldn't guess from his verses, he scored
high again (a 6 and a 7 – 7 the highest possible!)

in Amativeness (sexual love) and Adhesiveness
(friendship, brotherly love) when before his death
his head was read. He earned only a 5 for Poetic Faculties,
but that 5, pulled and pushed by his other numbers,
allowed our father of poesy to lay down some words
in the proper order on the page. That our nation

does not care does not matter, much.
That his modest federal job was taken from him,
and thus his pension, does not matter at all.
And that his brain was dropped and shattered, a cosmos,
on the floor, matters even less.

Bodo

History is largely made of Bodos.

EILEEN POWER, Medieval People

We could weep for him
but we won't: the man
who scythed and ground the oats
but ate no bread; who pumped one oar
among thousands at Lepanto, ocean
up to his clavicles and rising; who
in countless numbers served as food
for countless fish. The man,
or sometimes woman, three or four rows back
in the crowd (listless, slack-mouthed),
who lined the street when an army,
depleted or fat with loot, came home;
or the man behind such columns,
who gathered the dung
to sell or to pick for seeds. All the pig farmers,
rat catchers, charcoal burners, tanners
in their stink, root diggers living
in the next village over from the smallest village;
who thickened their soup with sawdust
or meal gathered from dirt
around the grindstone.
Your great-great-etc.-uncle Fedor who never spoke
but in grunts, who beat his spavined horse,
who beat his rented field
for millet, sorghum, who ate a chicken once a year,
who could not read
nor even sign an *X*; the slaves
unnamed who never made it
to the slavers, buzzards' bait,
or did not survive the crossing
if they did. All the Bodos
who stood on docks with breaking backs

and did not wave
and did not know Marco Polo
was setting out again; the zealous priest
eleventh on the list
to seek out Prester John; the convict-colonists
who preferred the gaol at home
but had no choice. The slug-pickers;
the sailors who bailed the bilge water
hanging by their heels; the doughboy
dead of typhus before he wrote a letter home;
the man who thought he pleased a minor Nazi
with an act of small servility
and was proud and told his wife and son;
who lost a leg and half his face for his king,
and then was cheated on his pension
and was not bitter. The man, the woman, who hanged
or burned for nothing
and did not weep, or, tortured, confessed
too fast for less; who praised his slop
in which a fish head floated....

Floating Baby Paintings

I like the paintings by the Venetian painters
(Titian, say, or Tintoretto, the Bellinis)
in question: large, dramatic canvases,
figurative (no abstract monkey business here),
relentlessly biblical. The Bible tells
a story, allegory, these guys paint it. Nice. Aside
from beauty, there's a purpose
to this work: people look, they've heard,
or sometimes read, the Bible stories
and they understand them better – the pictorial,
no doubt about it, is powerful. Words

about some gruesome (Christ on the Cross, thorns,
spikes splitting cartilage, spear,
vinegar-sponge in spearhole) or uplifting
(Resurrection) scene
are all right, but an image – there it is,
friend, that's what it looked like – better still.
The less than literal touches I like best,
however, in so many of these: the chubby,
ubiquitous, usually just hovering
above and/or back a bit
from the central tableau (we can see them,

but can the characters in the picture?) rosy fellows
with wings; joyous, busy,
observational little blimps, their delicate wings
not flapping (never painted as a blur
despite their weight), but there they fly, floating

babies! For centuries
they show up – sometimes carrying a lyre,
a dove or two, of course a bow,
but mostly just ecstatic, naked, fat.
Bless them, their cargo,
their unexampled flight patterns.

The Garden

The basic metaphor is good: blend dead,
redolent things – dried blood,
steamed bone meal, dried hoof and horn
meal, slag, dolomite,
bat guano – into the dirt,
wait; live things will emerge.
In between, of course, you insert a seed.
So fragile, at first – I examine rows
of lettuce seedlings with a reading glass,
their green so barely green
they break your heart. The only
tools you need are Stone Age
but made of metal: I love
the shovel's cut when you plunge
it in: the shiny, smooth cliff-face
and some worms (your garden's pals!)
in the middle of their bodies,
their lives, divided.... A rake,
a hoe, peasant tools,
but mostly you pick, pull, pinch by hand,
the green stains and stinks clinging
to your fingertips.
Don't read books about it,
or not many. Turn the dirt
and comb it smooth.
Plant what you like to eat.
Feed the birds – but not so much
that they get lazy –
and they will eat the bugs,
who should get their share,
but not one leaf of basil more.
It's all a matter of spirit, balance,
common cruel sense: something dies,
something's born, and, in the meantime,
you eat some salad.

Upon Seeing an Ultrasound Photo of an Unborn Child

Tadpole, it's not time yet to nag you
about college (though I have some thoughts
on that), baseball (ditto), or abstract
principles. Enjoy your delicious,
soupy womb-warmth, do some rolls and saults
(it'll be too crowded soon), delight in your early
dreams – which no one will attempt to analyse.
For now: may your toes blossom, your fingers
lengthen, your sexual organs grow (too soon
to tell which yet) sensitive, your teeth
form their buds in their forming jawbone, your already
booming heart expand (literally
now, metaphorically later); O your spine,
eyebrows, nape, knees, fibulae,
lungs, lips... But your soul,
dear child: I don't see it here, when
does that come in, whence? Perhaps God,
and your mother, and even I – we'll all contribute
and you'll learn yourself to coax it
from wherever: your soul, which holds your bones
together and lets you live
on earth. – Fingerling, sidecar, nubbin,
I'm waiting, it's me, Dad,
I'm out here. You already know
where Mom is. I'll see you more direcdy
upon arrival. You'll recognise
me – I'll be the tall-seeming, delighted
blond guy, and I'll have
your nose.

A Little Tooth

Your baby grows a tooth, then two,
and four, and five, then she wants some meat
directly from the bone. It's all

over: she'll learn some words, she'll fall
in love with cretins, dolts, a sweet
talker on his way to jail. And you,

your wife, get old, flyblown, and rue
nothing. You did, you loved, your feet
are sore. It's dusk. Your daughter's tall.

Great Advances in Vanity

Major progress is: in the act of embracing ourselves
we do not do so because of cold, fear,
but out of absolute – which is healthy,
the magazines say – self-love, which is healthy,
a positive self-image is *healthy*,

all the experts say,
and less effort
than loving an other. I am I, therefore
I am good: love thyself
selflessly, that's OK. And if

you want me, or want me
to want you, or want to
sell me something, then tell me
I'm beautiful. If there is a blank anywhere
in your life, an abyss tucked high up behind your breast bone,

or a black molecule of doubt
in your soul, well then,
fill in that blank,
palimpsest that abyss, that doubt with optimism: you can!
In the mirror in the morning say

this: *I like* my*self.* This
is your iambic dimeter mantra, say it,
and all the rest that diminishes you
will disappear down the bones of your face,
will die all night outside your door,

will file away like a line of ants.
Say it, say it: I'm beautiful,
I'm loved – and then wager it all,
all of the ice, all of it,
on the ice to win.

Split Horizon

(1994)

The People of the Other Village

hate the people of this village
and would nail our hats
to our heads for refusing in their presence to remove them
or staple our hands to our foreheads
for refusing to salute them
if we did not hurt them first: mail them packages of rats,
mix their flour at night with broken glass.
We do this, they do that.
They peel the larynx from one of our brothers' throats.
We de-vein one of their sisters.
The quicksand pits they built were good.
Our amputation teams were better.
We trained some birds to steal their wheat.
They sent to us exploding ambassadors of peace.
They do this, we do that.
We canceled our sheep imports.
They no longer bought our blankets.
We mocked their greatest poet
and when that had no effect
we parodied the way they dance
which did cause pain, so they, in turn, said our God
was leprous, hairless.
We do this, they do that.
Ten thousand (10,000) years, ten thousand
(10,000) brutal, beautiful years.

An Horatian Notion

The thing gets made, gets built, and you're the slave
who rolls the log beneath the block, then another,
then pushes the block, then pulls a log
from the rear back to the front
again and then again it goes beneath the block,
and so on. It's how a thing gets made – not
because you're sensitive, or you get genetic-lucky,
or God says: Here's a nice family,
seven children, let's see: this one in charge
of the village dunghill, these two die of buboes, this one
Kierkegaard, this one a drooling

nincompoop, this one clerk, this one cooper.
You need to love the thing you do – birdhouse building,
painting tulips exclusively, whatever – and then
you do it
so consciously driven
by your unconscious
that the thing becomes a wedge
that splits a stone and between the halves
the wedge then grows, i.e., the thing
is solid but with a soul,
a life of its own. Inspiration, the donnée,

the gift, the bolt of fire
down the arm that makes the art?
Grow up! Give me, please, a break!
You make the thing because you love the thing
and you love the thing because someone else loved it
enough to make you love it.
And with that your heart like a tent peg pounded
toward the earth's core.
And with that your heart on a beam burns
through the ionosphere.
And with that you go to work.

The Neighborhood of Make-Believe

To go there: do not fall asleep, your forehead
on the footstool; do not have
your lunchpail dreams
or dreams so peaceful you hear leaves thud
into the fine silt at a river's edge;
do not hope you'll find it on this updraft
or that downdraft
in the airy airlessness.
It is elsewhere, elsewhere, the neighborhood you seek.
The neighborhood you long for,
where the gentle trolley – *ding, ding* – passes
through, where the adults are kind
and, better, sane,
that neighborhood is gone, no, never
existed, though it should have
and had a chance once
in the hearts of women, men (farmers dreamed
this place, and teachers, book writers, oh thousands
of workers, mothers prayed for it, hunchbacks,
nurses, blind men, maybe most of all soldiers,
even a few generals, millions
through the millennia…), some of whom,
despite anvils on their chests,
despite taking blow after blow across shoulders and necks,
despite derision and scorn,
some of whom still, *still*
stand up every day against ditches swollen with blood,
against ignorance, still dreaming,
full-fledged adults, still fighting,
trying to build a door to that place,
trying to pry open the ugly,
bullet-pocked, and swollen gate
to the other side,
the neighborhood of make-believe.

Amiel's Leg

We were in a room that was once an attic,
tops of trees filled the windows, a breeze
crossed the table where we sat
and Amiel, about age four, came to visit
with her father, my friend,
and it was spring I think, and I remember
being happy – her mother was there too,
and my wife, and a few other friends.
It was spring, late spring, because the trees
were full but still that slightly lighter
green; the windows were open,
some of them, and I'll say it
out loud: I was happy, sober, at the time childless
myself, and it was one
of those moments: just like that, Amiel
climbed on my lap and put her head back against my chest.
I put one hand on her knees
and my other hand on top of that hand.
That was all, that was it.
Amiel's leg was cool, faintly rubbery.
We were there – I wish I knew the exact
date, time – and that
was all, that was it.

Frankly, I Don't Care

This miserable scene demands a groan.

JOHN GAY

Frankly, I don't care if the billionaire is getting divorced
and thus boosting the career
of his girlfriend, a 'model/spokesperson' with no job
and nothing to promote; nor does my concern
over celebrity X undergoing surgical procedures,
leaked as 'primarily cosmetic' if it can be measured
quantitatively, reach the size of the space
inside a hollow needle. Regardless,
prayer vigils are being held
around the clock in the hospital lobby.
It's not that I wish
for a slip of the surgeon's wrist
but I just flat-simple don't care
although I understand and try
to empathise: as beauty diminishes
so does the bankroll. I am also indifferent
to – to the point of yawns large enough
to swallow the world – a senator's or, say, singer's
girlfriend's or boyfriend's disclosures
re the singer's or senator's sexual behavior – well, unless
the disclosure is *explicitly* detailed
and for christsake *interesting!*
– But does this protest too much?
We the people, day-laboring citizens, need to love
those of you larger than us, those whose teeth
are like floodlights against loneliness,
whose great gifts of song, or for joke telling,
or thespianly sublime transformations
take us, for whole moments at a time, away
from ourselves. We need
you and from this point on we promise
to respect your privacy,

diminish our demands on you,
never to take pleasure
in your troubles or pain.
And on those cruel days when death has its way
and takes two or even three of you
at once, three of more or less equal fame, we will,
in the obituaries, the newscasts, the front pages,
we will list your departures alphabetically;
your popularity will not, on this day, be tallied
or polled. Because in death, although still not anonymous,
you will be like us: small,
equal, voiceless, and gone.

Endive

If I mix a vegetable and moral metaphor
then this pale,
arrogant little leaf– its juices spare,
its taste pinched
and numbing – is equivalent
to a rich child pulling legs
off a bug, to a swaggering walk through a TB ward
by a pulmonary giant. Not to mention
a pathetic excuse for salad: four, five spiked shards
arranged like spokes
around its hub: a radish delicately carved.
The white plate upon which it sits so bare it blinds me.
Who, forced to wear white butler's gloves,
bends over a row all day
to pick this for a lousy wage
and can't afford or, I'd prefer, refuses
to eat it? It's so pallid
turning to yellow, I feel stabbing it
with my fork
would hurt it
or at least be impolite
so I slide the shiny tines beneath a piece
and lift it to my lips
and it's as if I'm eating air
but with a slight afterburn: dust and bone,
privilege and toe dancing.
So delicate, curling in on itself
in an ultimate self-embrace: fussy, bitter, chaste, clerical
little leaf.

The Driver Ant

Every member of the army is completely blind.
JOHN COMPTON, on the driver ant

Eats meat exclusively. Can't bear
direct sunlight, marches at night,
in tall grass, or in covered causeways
it builds, by day. Relentless,
nervous, short, conservative,
twenty million or more,
like a thick black living rope
they exit, often, the colony
to eat: lizards, guanas, monkeys,
rats, mice, the tasty
largest python, *Python natelensis*,
who just devoured a small antelope
and can't move: double dinner,
in a few hours a pile of bones
inside a pile of bones.
This army's slow
(one meter per three min.) so
they can't catch you
unless you're lame,
or dumb, or staked
to the ground – a hard way to die,
eating first your eyes,
and then too many mandibles
clean you to your spine.
The Driver Ant, penniless,
goes out to eat
in hordes, in rivers, in armies of need,
good citizens
serving a famished state.

Kalashnikov

(an AK-47 assault rifle, probably the most
numerous small-arms weapon in history)

Designed by Mikhail Kalashnikov who, if alive
today, is seventy-three years old,
but is he
as well known in his native Russia
as Marina Tsvetayeva, Anna Akhmatova,
or Osip Mandelstam? Russians love
their poets. I don't know

how they feel about Kalashnikov
but he is or was wealthier
than the poets above ever were
and has out there several million
of his namesakes: read a book
in which people shoot people – revolutionaries,
whether earnest, sincere,

or just thugs: Kalashnikovs, everybody's got one.
There's a guerrilla
somewhere: a Kalashnikov. Assassins,
warlords' soldiers, smugglers, pirates,
poachers: Kalashnikovs, caliber
7.62 x 39, 600 rounds
per minute, a potential 10 corpses

per second.
Kalashnikov – it's not a dance,
nor a troupe of funny jugglers,
nor is it a vodka,
and if you said a small city (pop. 49,000)
in the southern Crimea,
you'd be stone-dead wrong.

Money

A paper product. We say it's green
but it's not, it's slate green, drained green.
New, it smells bad
but we like to sniff it
and when we have a relative pile
we not only want to inhale it but also look at it,
hear it buzz
as we work with our thumbs
its corners like a deck of cards.
A wall of it would be nice, in bricks
like you see in the movies
when vaults get robbed.
And those beautiful – so tiny – red, blue threads,
capillaries, cilia, embedded
in the texture of the paper (that secret
which most thwarts the phony money men),
those threads
like river valleys on a distant planet,
rivers with no end, no source,
like steep ravines in an otherwise flat pan
of a landscape. Look long
and deep enough
at a piece of paper money
and you will see the heaven you were promised,
there, which we look so hard into,
to the very bottom, depths of which
we are called
by the riverbed, the ravine's bleached stones
calling us down: money, money,
paper money.

The Big Picture

gets made up of 5.3 billion little pictures (sacks, thousands,
of rice rotting, rat-gnawed, in warehouses, jail cell
graffiti, a tiny crimson powder-burned disc
on a man's forehead, a torturer's migraine, immense
abstract delusions – *no problem here* – a filthy

fingernail sunk in a chunk of gray bread...), eleven pictures
of medium size (the Marxist discussion group
breaks down into smaller groups
to study punctuational/syntactical nuances, why nobody
minds lies if they are colossal enough, etc.), a few blank

frames (example: Jesus walking on water and rising
from the dead?, the Mormon guy, Joe Smith – sounds like
an alias – digging up some gold plates
in his backyard?: this enumeration, this list
of mysteries could go on and on

without *ever any* verification...), a few ruined
snapshots (a chicken in every BBQ, social justice), one
shattered vision, a few mild
auditory hallucinations, faint harp
music, celestial crowing

or choiring, or the low love cooing
of an amorous duo,
Ignorance and Certainty, that each lost one of us,
I pray, would agree, should agree, should be
sterilised!

Grim Town in a Steep Valley

This valley: as if a huge, dull, primordial ax
once slammed into the earth
and then withdrew, innumerable millennia ago.
A few flat acres
ribbon either side of the river sliding sluggishly
past the clock tower, the convenience store.
If a river could look over its shoulder,
glad to be going, this one would.
In town center: a factory of clangor and stink,
of grinding and oil,
hard howls from drill bits
biting sheets of steel. All my brothers
live here, every cousin, many dozens
of sisters, my worn aunts
and numb uncles, the many many of me,
a hundred sad wives,
all of us countrymen and -women
born next to each other behind the plow
in this valley, each of us
pressing to our chests a loaf of bread
and a jug of milk.... The river is low
this time of year and the bedstones' blackness
marks its lack
of depth. A shopping cart
lies on its side in center stream
gathering branches, detritus, silt,
forcing the already weak current to part for it,
dividing it, but even so diminished
it's glad to be going,
glad to be gone.

River Blindness (Onchocerciasis)

First, a female buffalo gnat of the genus *Simulium* bites you
and in the process
deposits her infective larvae.
In ten to twenty months (no big hurry) they grow
to threadlike adult worms
which live up to fifteen years under the skin,
intermuscularly, in fascial planes, against capsules
of joints or the shafts of long bones – the neighborhoods
they love inside you. The adult females,
now residing in your body, produce live embryos
which live a year or two,
migrating, restless,
during which time they will likely invade your eyes,
lymph glands, or other (you don't want to know
which) organs. Results
are unpleasant: blindness, which might be merciful
for then you don't see: rash, wheals, gross
lichenification, atrophy (known as "lizard skin"),
enlarged lymph glands
leading to pockets of loose flesh,
"hanging groins", which predispose
to hernia, and so on.
Treatment: Serious drugs, some so toxic the treatment worse
than the illness.
Prognosis: If you are not reinfected, the parasites die out
within fifteen years. Symptoms of disease, however, may
get worse during this time.
Prevention: Avoid Third World communities,
particularly those located within twenty kilometers
of fast-flowing rivers
in which *Simulium* prefers to breed.
Some twenty to forty million (hard to be exact!) people
infected,
baby flies dying, dying
in their eyes,
blinding them.

History Books

That is, their authors, leave out
one thing: the smell. How sour, no, rancid – bad cheese
and sweat – the narrow corridors of Hitler's bunker
during the last days powdered
by plaster shaken down
under bomb after bomb. Or (forward or backward
through time, history books take you) downstream
a mile or two from a river-crossing ambush
a corpse washes ashore
or catches in branches
and bloats in the sun. The carrion eaters
who do not fly
come by their noses: the thick,
ubiquitous, sick, sweet smell.
Most of history, however,
is banal, not bloody: the graphite and wood smell
of a pencil factory, the glue- fertiliser- paper-
(oh redolent!) shoe- hat- (ditto malodor
and poisonous) chemical- salt cod-
munitions- canning- shirtwaist- plastics- box-
tractor- etc. factories – and each one
peopled by people: groins, armpits, feet.
A bakery, during famine; guards, smoking, by the door.
Belowdecks, two years out, dead calm, tropics.
And wind a thousand miles all night combing
the tundra: chilled grasses, polar bear droppings,
glacial exhalations.... Open
the huge book of the past: *whoosh!*: a staggering cloud
of stinks, musks
and perfumes, swollen pheromones, almond
and anise, offal dumps, mass graves exhumed, flower
heaps, sandalwood bonfires, milk vapors
from a baby's mouth, all of us
wading hip-deep through the endless
waftings, one bottomless soup
of smells: primal, atavistic – sniff, sniff, sniff.

Shaving the Graveyard

The graveyard being what he called his face;
even as a young man
he called his face the graveyard – he talked
like that, funny, odd
things that scared me sometimes

in our early years. I thought maybe he was a little touched
(his Uncle Bob was certifiable)
but it was just his way of talking. *U-feeisms*,
he told me once, he liked to use *u-feeisms*,
which was no language

I ever heard of. He never touched a drop, though,
nor ever lifted a hand against me
or the kids, and when it came to loving,
well, he was sweet, but talking strange then
too: Bug Sauce, he'd call me, or Lavender Limbs,

or sometimes Birdbath – never Honey
or Sugar like other husbands when they talked, talked.
He was funny like that. Anyway,
after breakfast (he always shaved *after* breakfast,
said his face was 'looser' then)

he'd stroke his chin and say:
Time to shave the graveyard,
and he would and then he'd go to work,
the handle of his lunchpail hooked through
with a belt and slung

over his shoulder. Some days I'd watch him
until he reached the corner
of Maple and Cottage
where he turned and walked the two blocks
to the mill.

Pecked to Death by Swans

(for Stephen Dobyns)

Your tear-wracked family bedside: elderly grandchildren,
great-grandchildren arriving
straight from med school; not a peep of pain, calm,
lucid, last words impeccably drafted?

No. Pecked to death by swans.

Having saved the lives of twelve crippled children
(pulled from a burning circus tent), the president
calling your hospital room, and you say: *Tell him*
to call back; all the opiate drugs you want?

No. Pecked to death by swans.

Great honors accrued, *Don't go* telegram from the pope
on the side table, serious lobby
already in place re a commemorative stamp; a long
long life capped by falling, peacefully, asleep?

No. I said: Pecked to death by swans.

By a bullet meant for a lover or a best friend,
by a car set to kill someone else whom you pushed,
because you could, out of the way; the ululations
of a million mourners rising to your window?

No. Pecked to death by swans.

Autobiographical

The minute my brother gets out of jail I want
some answers: when our mother
murdered our father
did she find out first, did he tell her – the pistol's tip
parting his temple's fine hairs – did he
tell her where our sister (the youngest, Alice)
hid the money Grandma (mother's side)
stole from her Golden Age Group?
It was a lot of money but *enough to die for?*
was what Mom said she asked him,
giving him a choice. *I'll see you in hell,*
she said Dad said
and then she said (this is in the trial transcript): *Not*
any time soon, needle dick!
We know Alice hid the money – she was arrested

a week later in Tacoma for armed robbery,
which she would not have done
if she had it. Alice was (she died
of a heroin overdose six hours after making bail)
syphilitic, stupid, and rude
but not greedy. So she hid the money,
or Grandma did,
but since her stroke can't say a word,
doesn't seem to know anybody.
Doing a dime at Dannemora
for an unrelated sex crime, my brother
might know something but won't answer
my letters, refuses to see me,
though he was the one who called me
at divinity school
after Mom was arrested. He could hardly
get the story out from laughing
so much: Dad had missed
his third in a row the day before with his parole officer,

the cops were sent
to pick him up (*Bad timing*, said Mom) and found him
before he was cold.
He was going back to jail anyway, Mom said,
said the cops,
which they could and did use against her
to the tune of double digits, which means,
what with the lupus, she's guaranteed
to die inside. Ask her?
She won't talk to me.
She won't give me the time of day.

Emily's Mom

(Emily Norcross Dickinson, 1804–1882,
mother of Emily Elizabeth Dickinson, 1830-1886)

Today we'd say she was depressed, clinically. Then,
they called it 'nameless disabling apathy', 'persistent nameless
infirmity', 'often she fell sick
with nameless illnesses and wept
with quiet resignation'. *The Nameless*, they should
have called it! She was *depressed*,
unhappy, and who can blame her
given her husband, Edward, who was, without exception,
absent – literally and otherwise – and in comparison
to a glacial range, cooler by a few degrees.
Febrile, passionate: not Edward.
'From the first she was desolately lonely.'
A son gets born, a daughter (the poet), another daughter,
and that's all, then nearly fifty years
of 'tearful withdrawal and obscure maladies'.
She was depressed, for christsake! The Black Dog
got her, the Cemetery Sledge, the Airless Vault,
it ate her up
and her options few: no Prozac then, no Elavil,
couldn't eat *all* the rum cake,
divorce the sluggard?
Her children? Certainly they
brought her some joy?: 'I always ran home to Awe
when a child, if anything befell me. He was an Awful Mother,
but I liked him better than none.'
This is what her daughter, the poet, said.
No, it had her,
for a good part of a century
it had her by the neck: the Gray Python,
the Vortex Vacuum.
During the last long (seven) years,
crippled further by a stroke,

it did not let go but, *but*: 'We were never intimate
Mother and children while she was our Mother
but mines in the ground meet by tunneling
and when she became our Child, the Affection came.'
This is what Emily, her daughter, wrote
in that manner wholly hers,
the final word
on Emily, her mother – melancholic,
fearful, starved-of-love.

'Mr John Keats Five Feet Tall' Sails Away

on the *Maria Crowther*,
a cargo brig
of 127 tons bound for Italy,
Naples, the sun
which was thought would cure his cough, his lungs.
The day: Sunday, 17 September 1820.
With him: Severn,
a painter, his nurse-companion;
Mrs Pidgeon, a pain in the ass
and cold; Miss Cotterell,
like Keats consumptive
and 'very lady-like but a sad martyr
to her illness,' wrote Severn;
the captain and crew.
This was not a pleasure cruise.
Second day out: the sick
and nonsick get seasick
and 'bequeath to the mighty sea their breakfasts'.
Storms, water by the pailful
in the sleeping cabin; calms, nary a puff.
A squall (Bay of Biscay),
a calm again (Cape Saint Vincent),
then, one dawn, Gibraltar, the African coast!
Then, Bay of Naples,
Saturday, 21 October – ten days
quarantined
during which not one porthole opened
it rained so hard and long.
Welcome, Mr Keats, to sunny southern Italy.
Then, by wagon, on roads ripe
with malaria, to Rome
from where in the two months plus
he still has lungs
he does not write again to Fanny Brawne,
whom he loves,

though he does write about
her to a friend
the famous sentence: 'Oh God! God! God!' (in whom
he had no faith) 'Every thing
I have in my trunk
reminds me of her
and goes through me like a spear.'
And the better but less quoted
next sentence: 'The silk
lining she put in my travelling cap scalds
my head.' The verb choice 'scalds'
perfect here (literally he had the fever,
figuratively...), the tactility
fresher, the melodrama cut
by an almost comic hyperbole. It is
more Keats than Keats,
who died 172 years, 8 months, 2 weeks, and 4 days
ago – this tiny man
John Keats,
who wrote some poems
without which,
inch by inch – in broken
barn light,
in classrooms (even there!),
under the lamp where what you read
teaches you what you love – without which
we would each,
inch by hammered inch,
we would each
be diminished.

'I Love You Sweatheart'

A man risked his life to write the words.
A man hung upside down (an idiot friend
holding his legs?) with spray paint
to write the words on a girder fifty feet above
a highway. And his beloved,
the next morning driving to work...?
His words are not (meant to be) so unique.
Does she recognise his handwriting?
Did he hint to her at her doorstep the night before
of 'something special, darling, tomorrow'?
And did he call her at work
expecting her to faint with delight
at his celebration of her, his passion, his risk?
She will *know* I love her now,
the *world* will know my love for her!
A man risked his life to write the words.
Love is like this at the bone, we hope, love
is like this, Sweatheart, all sore and dumb
and dangerous, ignited, blessed – always,
regardless, no exceptions,
always in blazing matters like these: blessed.

NEW POEMS FROM

New and Selected Poems

(1997)

Refrigerator, 1957

More like a vault – you pull the handle out
and on the shelves: not a lot,
and what there is (a boiled potato
in a bag, a chicken carcass
under foil) looking dispirited,
drained, mugged. This is not
a place to go in hope or hunger.
But, just to the right of the middle
of the middle door shelf, on fire, a lit-from-within red,
heart red, sexual red, wet neon red,
shining red in their liquid, exotic,
aloof, slumming
in such company: a jar
of maraschino cherries. Three-quarters
full, fiery globes, like strippers
at a church social. Maraschino cherries, maraschino,
the only foreign word I knew. Not once
did I see these cherries employed: not
in a drink, nor on top
of a glob of ice cream,
or just pop one in your mouth. Not once.
The same jar there through an entire
childhood of dull dinners – bald meat,
pocked peas and, see above,
boiled potatoes. Maybe
they came over from the old country,
family heirlooms, or were status symbols
bought with a piece of the first paycheck
from a sweatshop,
which beat the pig farm in Bohemia,
handed down from my grandparents
to my parents
to be someday mine,
then my child's?

They were beautiful
and, if I never ate one,
it was because I knew it might be missed
or because I knew it would not be replaced
and because you do not eat
that which rips your heart with joy.

Criss Cross Apple Sauce

(for Claudia)

Criss cross apple sauce
do me a favor and get lost
while you're at it drop dead
then come back without a head
my daughter sings for me
when I ask her what she learned in school today
as we drive from her mother's house to mine.
She knows I like some things that rhyme.
She sings another she knows I like:
Trick or treat, trick or treat
give me something good to eat
if you don't I don't care
I'll put apples in your underwear....
Apples in your underwear – I like that more
than Lautréamont's umbrella
on the operating table, I say to her
and ask her if she sees the parallel.
She says no but she prefers the apples too.
Sitting on a bench
nothing to do
along come some boys – p.u., p.u., p.u.
my daughter sings,
my daughter with her buffalo-size heart,
my daughter brilliant and kind,
my daughter singing
as we drive from her mother's house to mine.

The Voice You Hear When You Read Silently

is not silent, it is a speaking-
out-loud voice in your head: it is *spoken*,
a voice is *saying* it
as you read. It's the writer's words,
of course, in a literary sense
his or her voice, but the sound
of that voice is the sound of your voice.
Not the sound your friends know
or the sound of a tape played back
but your voice
caught in the dark cathedral
of your skull, your voice heard
by an internal ear informed by internal abstracts
and what you know by feeling,
having felt. It is your voice
saying, for example, the word barn
that the writer wrote
but the barn you say
is a barn you know or knew. The voice
in your head, speaking as you read,
never says anything neutrally – some people
hated the barn they knew,
some people love the barn they know
so you hear the word loaded
and a sensory constellation
is lit: horse-gnawed stalls,
hayloft, black heat tape wrapping
a water pipe, a slippery
spilled chirr of oats from a split sack,
the bony, filthy haunches of cows....
And barn is only a noun – no verb
or subject has entered into the sentence yet!
The voice you hear when you read to yourself
is the clearest voice: you speak it
speaking to you.

This Space Available

You could put an *X* here.
You could draw a picture of a horse.
You could write a tract,
manifesto – but keep it short.
You could wail, whine,
rail or polysyllable celebrate.
You could fill this space
with one syllable: praise.
The only requirement,
the anti-poet said,
is to improve upon the blank page,
which, if you are not made blind
by ego, is a hard task.
You could write some numbers here.
You could write your name, and dates.
You could leave a thumbprint,
or paint your lips and kiss the page.
A hard task – the blank
so creamy, a cold
and perfect snowfield upon which
a human, it's only human,
wants to leave
his inky black and awkward marks.

Commercial Leech Farming Today

(for Robert Sacherman)

Although it never rivaled wheat, soybean,
cattle and so on farming
there was a living
in leeches
and after a period of decline
there is again
a living to be made
from this endeavor: they're used to reduce
the blood in tissues
after plastic surgery – eyelifts, tucks,
wrinkle erad, or in certain
microsurgeries – reattaching a finger, penis.
I love the capitalist
spirit. As in most businesses
the technology has improved: instead
of driving an elderly horse
into a leech pond, letting him die
by exsanguination,
and hauling him out
to pick the bloated blossoms
from his hide, it's now done at Biopharm
(the showcase operation in Swansea,
Wales) – temp control, tanks, aerator
pumps, several species,
each for a specific job. Once, 19th century,
they were applied to the temple
as a treatment for mental
illness. Today we know
their exact chemistry: hirudin,
a blood thinner in their saliva,
also an anesthesia
and dilators for the wound area.
Don't you love
the image: the Dr lays a leech along

the tiny stitches of an eyelift.
Where they go after their work is done
I don't know
but I've heard no complaints
from Animal Rights
so perhaps they're retired
to a lake or adopted
as pets, maybe the best looking
kept to breed. I don't know. I like the story,
I like the going backwards
to ignorance
to come forward to vanity. I like
the small role they can play
in beauty
or the reattachment of a part,
I like the story because it's true.

A Small Tin Parrot Pin

Next to the tiny bladeless windmill
of a salt shaker
on the black tablecloth
is my small tin parrot pin,
bought from a bin,
75 cents, cheap, not pure tin – an alloy,
some plastic toy tin?
The actual pin, the pin that pins the pin,
will fall off soon
and thus the parrot,
if I wear it, which I will,
on my lapel. I'll look down
and it'll be gone.
Let it be found by a child,
or someone sad, eyes
on the sidewalk, or what a prize
it would be for a pack rat's nest.
My parrot's paint
is vivid: his head's red, bright yellow of breast
and belly, a strip of green,
then purple, a soft
creamy purple, then bright – you know
the color – parrot green
wing feathers. Tomorrow I think
I'll wear it on my blue coat.
Tonight, someone whom I love
sleeps in the next room,
the room next to the room with the black tablecloth,
the salt shaker, the parrot pin.
She was very sleepy
and less impressed than I
with my parrot
with whom, with which I
am very pleased.

The Street of Clocks

(2001)

The fact is the sweetest dream labour knows.

ROBERT FROST

I am certain of nothing but the holiness of the Heart's
affections and the truth of the Imagination.

JOHN KEATS

Cucumber Fields Crossed by High-Tension Wires

The high-tension spires spike the sky
beneath which boys bend
to pick from prickly vines
the deep-sopped fruit, the rind's green
a green sunk
in green. They part the plants' leaves,
reach into the nest,
and pull out mother, father, fat Uncle Phil.
The smaller yellow-green children stay,
for now. The fruit goes
in baskets by the side of the row,
every thirty feet or so. By these bushels
the boys get paid, in cash,
at day's end, this summer
of the last days of the empire
that will become known as
the past, adoios, *then*,
the ragged-edged beautful blink.

The Man into Whose Yard You Should Not Hit Your Ball

each day mowed
and mowed his lawn, his dry quarter-acre,
the machine slicing a wisp
from each blade's tip. Dust storms rose
around the roar, 6 P.M. every day,
spring, summer, fall. If he could mow
the snow he would.
On one side, his neighbours the cows
turned their backs to him
and did what they do to the grass.
Where he worked, I don't know,
but it set his jaw to: tight.
His wife a cipher, shoebox tissue,
a shattered apron. As if
into her head he drove a wedge of shale.
Years later, his daughter goes to jail.
Mow, mow, mow his lawn
gently down a decade's summers.
On his other side lived mine and me,
across a narrow pasture, often fallow –
a field of fly balls, the best part of childhood
and baseball. But if a ball crossed his line,
as one did in 1956
and another in 1958,
it came back coleslaw – his lawnmower
ate it up, happy
to cut something, no matter
what the manual said
about foreign objects, stones, or sticks.

Plague Victims Catapulted over Walls into Besieged City

Early germ
warfare. The dead
hurled this way turn like wheels
in the sky. Look: there goes
Larry the Shoemaker, barefoot, over the wall,
and Mary Sausage Stuffer, see how she flies,
and the Hatter twins, both at once, soar
over the parapet, little Tommy's elbow bent
as if in a salute,
and his sister, Mathilde, she follows him,
arms outstretched, through the air,
just as she did on earth.

Bonehead

Bonehead time, bonehead town. Bonehead teachers.
Bonehead mom, bonehead dad, bonehead aunts
and uncles and cousins too.
Bonehead me, bonehead you.
Bonehead books, playground, box lunch, fast food,
tract homes, Sunday school.
Bonehead Truman, McCarthy, Eisenhower too.
Bonehead me, bonehead you.
Bonehead music, TV, H-bomb, movies,
butch cut, tail fins, baby boom.
Bonehead Russia, America, England too.
Bonehead me, bonehead you.

In the Bedroom Above the Embalming Room

a man sits on the bed's edge in a white T-shirt,
white socks. He is my neighbour,
the local undertaker.
His wife lies behind him, reading a book,
the sheet drawn up above her breasts.
Otherwise, it would be impolite to look.
Or to look I'd wait until they dressed.
From my window they make a kind of X.
I've seen her feed the birds,
but not so much they stay
too long and leave their lime
to stain her deck and waste her time
in washing it away.

Thomas the Broken-Mouthed

A sack on his back, his burlap shirt flapping in a devil's wind,
Thomas the Broken-Mouthed
walks up and down
the bad land, and amidst the bad believers,
he was born in, and among.
He walks up and down, his big wooden stick striking
the road just ahead of the two still
unsettled puffs of dust
his bare feet raise. Thomas the Broken-Mouthed – called thus
for his lies, say some,
called thus for other reasons, some others say.
In each village two or three fall behind him – disaffected vendors
of drowsy syrups, stiff-fingered cutpurses, sour
camel drivers, well poisoners, and children (milky-skinned,
pockmarked), children of the rich,
of prelates, pushing before them
wooden-wheeled barrows of grain
to bake into bread
to eat on the march. Thomas the Broken-Mouthed has a mission,
within which is a vision,
within which
is a tiny black fire. *Who will pile the drought-dried straw on this fire,*
who will be the naphtha resin,
who will follow the fire,
who will be the sparks with fiery wings for me? asks
Thomas the Broken-Mouthed,
standing on a tree stump that reveals
one hundred rings, one hundred years
that the books now call The Last One Hundred Years.

The Handsome Swamp

knows it's a handsome swamp: the alligators
tell it so, as do the water lilies (always
sycophantic) and their pads. The bug life
stands on its hind legs
and cheers. *Let's live in the handsome swamp!*
The feeders on fish
and the fish food, the oxygen-spewing algae,
the vines, the cypress
and its knees – all are glad.
And the handsome swamp
keeps its handsome up: combing its reeds,
silk-sieving its silt.
The thick black snakes love the handsome swamp.
They speak this to it
as they cruise in grids
on its surface. But now
the green tree frogs,
those of the bright spots on their backs,
sing *no, no, no*, contrarily, all night, *no, no, no*.
This stirs the macaws to clatter; a hornbill
picks a parasite
from beneath his wing
and cracks it with his beak, which sound catches
a big beetle's antennae, and then the monkeys
take up with it (it's always
the *me, me, me* monkeys, greedy
for personification), and finally the rats
come out, noses first,
and gather in pods,
sniffing the air.

Grain Burning Far Away

The wheat fields blaze, wide waving plains
of them, on fire again, the black burn-line lapping
the gold grain: nature's delete button eating
each letter of each stalk. Over that short mountain
to the north, barley fields ignite,
and to the south, across the salt marshes, acres
and acres of oats
crackle and smoke,
and, it is reported from the east, the long green stands of corn
sawed off at the ankles
by heat. All the flora's, in fact, on fire: onion fields fried
underground, not one turnip unscorched, every root,
bulb, and peanut on the planet boiled
in the soil. Trees burn
like matches, but faster, orchids die
when the fire's still a mile away. Seaweed, too,
and the kelp beds
from the top down blacken like candle wicks; spinach, in cans,
when opened, is ash. Moss melts,
hedgerows explode, every
green thing on earth
on fire and still all smoke jumpers snug,
asleep, undisturbed, the fire station's pole cold,
palmless, the fire extinguisher fat
with foam. Hear it snap,
the red angry fire,
hear it take the air and turn it into pain,
see the flame's blue, bruised heart
never waver, waver, never waver.

The Doldrum Fracture Zone

The place where sailors – though now open
to all professions – went to consider the mirage
of their own despair. Once, only sailors could
go there: the breezeless place,
the weed-choked and stinking sea plain
where they stalled for weeks, months. Today,
the Zone comes to us,
its great grey inertness dragged
like opaque knife wounds over each
who stands on a shore and calls it in,
dragged over him or her who believes his or her despair is
a mirage and not
a mirror.... That man
who still holds the handle of the mailbox open, its huge black mouth
having just swallowed
a letter that cannot be unwritten.
It falls on the top of a pile of other such letters
in their white dresses
in the dark – that man has called it in.
There is a sound of tiny roots being torn,
and a water spider, skating smoothly over the Zone's flat surface, sinks.

The Poison Shirt

You put it on to walk the bright day, dumb
to the little skull-
and-crossbones
buttons, dumb to pulmonary numbing, half-hazy eye, rubber
ankles, not
noticing the sound
of people slumping – *shhump* – to the sidewalk
three seconds
after you pass. Each moment slimmer than nil – so the day passes, too,
with its trail of the poisoned
that ends with the you
in the poison shirt.

A Bird, Whose Wingtips Were on Fire,

led the small boy, lost in the forest at night,
to the clearing's edge
where the search teams
were gathering to look for him.
He ran to his weeping mother and father,
who raised him in their arms,
and all gathered around in great joy – the neighbours,
the cops, soldiers,
sailors, field hands, blood-
hounds, the high school marching band, all
circled the boy in great joy until
he talked of the bird
that came to him as he sat shivering
beside a moss-graced boulder,
second night lost
in the woods. No one wanted to hear that,
even in their relief
no one wanted to believe
a bird with flaming wingtips
lit a path
and led the boy on it to safety. Better
that it was dumb luck or, as many murmur,
the will of a being
with a short one-syllable name.
What colour was the bird? Did it speak to you?,
they asked the boy. Grey-brown, said the boy,
and no, it didn't speak, birds
don't talk. Were you playing with matches,
and did you set a bird on fire
which then flew away,
and you followed?, they asked the boy.
No matches, no hunger,
the boy said, and the only things that scared me
were the orchids and a fawn.

Slimehead *(Hoplostethus atlanticus)*

Humans eat first with their ears, so
to sell this deep-sea fish
we give some poetry to its name: orange roughy.
Oh tasty, despite its mucus-exuding head – that's gone
long before your dinner plate. A mild meat,
firm, low fat,
fished a mile beneath the waves.
Slow-growing, long-lived: up to 150 years.
In the lightless depths
it's brown, not orange. When you pull it up
each blood vessel bursts,
in its version of the bends?
I ate it, twice.
I'll eat it again
when it's over being overfished, if so.
But rather than its flanks
sautéed in this or that,
I'd like to roll inside a shoal
of them, down there where nobody goes,
to know what they know,
to not know what I know,
down there with the hoki, hake,
rattail, oreo dory, my dear slimeheads
and their countrymen,
the shy, prolific squid.

Salve

Paint me with it,
he tells the nurse,
and calls, too, for balm,
ointment, slather it all
(and add some tincture) on him.
In the soft moth powder of it
swathe him, swathe him, on white sheets,
in a white room. Some unguent
on his clavicle, please, nurse,
and on each ventricle lotion would be good.
To each temple: assuagement.
To the bony comers of his eye sockets, your fingers,
nurse, to press there anodynes.
Pour a river (with rivulets)
of emollients from his nape
down his spine's valley – let a pool
fill there, a shallow pond
of salve, let it gather there,
then place a tiny boat
upon its eastern shore, nurse,
and launch it westward, gently, with your thumb.

Regarding (Most) Songs

Whatever is too stupid to say can be sung.
JOSEPH ADDISON (1672-1719)

The human voice can sing a vowel to break your heart.
It trills a string of banal words,
but your blood jumps, regardless. You don't care
about the words but only *how* they're sung
and the music behind – the brass, the drums.
Oh the primal, necessary drums
behind the words so dumb!
That power, the bang and the boom and again the bang
we cannot, need not, live without,
nor without other means to make that sweet noise,
the guitar or violin, the things that sing
the plaintive, joyful sounds.
Which is why I like songs best
when I can't hear the words, or, better still,
when there are no words at all.

A Library of Skulls

Shelves and stacks and shelves of skulls, a Dewey
decimal number inked on each unfurrowed forehead.
Here's a skull
who, before he lost his fleshy parts
and lower bones, once
walked beside a river (we're in the poetry section
now), his head full of love
and loneliness; and this smaller skull,
in the sociology stacks, smiling (they're all
smiling) – it's been empty
a hundred years. That slot
across another's temple? An axe blow
that fractured
her here. Look at this one from the children's shelves,
a baby, his fontanel
a screaming mouth and this time no teeth, no smile.
Here are a few (history): a murderer,
and this one – see how close their eye sockets! – a thief,
and here's a rack of torturers' skulls
beneath which a longer, much longer, row of the tortured.
And look: generals' row,
their epaulets
on the shelves to each side of them.
Shelves and shelves, stacks stacked on top of stacks,
floor above floor,
this towering high-rise library
of skulls, not another bone in the place,
and just now the squeak of a wheel
on a cart piled high with skulls
on their way back to shelves,
while in the next aisle
a cart is filling with those about to be loaned
to the tall, broken-hearted man waiting
at the desk, his library card
face down before him.

The Fish-Strewn Fields

After the river rose above its banks, after the farms
and fields and yards
were drowned and drained again, all
was fish-strewn, stump- and root-strewn,
besotted. Here and there,
pieces of an upriver town – light blue ice tray,
birdhouse, the town clerk – all litter the pastures.
Aerial photos (all is mud now, no water for boats,
no ground to walk on) show
us this, the helicopter dropping close
to look for anything alive.
The town clerk's blue shirt blooms.
He drank deep of the waters and mud.
The river recedes now, back between,
then below its banks,
and recedes still more, drains to the stones,
then through the bedrock beneath its sand, oh, it sinks,
the river, it's gone,
and then the banks close like the lips of a wound,
leaving a wormy scar
along the bottom of our valley
for miles, miles.

Unlike, for Example, the Sound of a Riptooth Saw

gnawing through a shinbone, a high howl
inside of which a bloody, slashed-by-growls note
is heard, unlike *that*
sound, and instead, its opposite: a barely sounded
sound (put your nuclear ears
on for it, your giant hearing horn, its cornucopia mouth
wide) – a slippery whoosh of rain
sliding down a mirror
leaned against a windfallen tree stump, the sound
a child's head makes
falling against his mother's breast,
or the sound, from a mile away, as the town undertaker
lets Grammy's wrist
slip from his grip
and fall to the shiny table. And, if you turn
your head just right
and open all your ears,
you might hear
this *finest* sound, this lost sound: a plough's silvery prow
cleaving the earth (your finger
dragging through milk, a razor
cutting silk) like a clipper ship cuts the sea.
If you do hear this sound,
then follow it with your ear and also your eye
as it and the tractor that pulls it
disappear over a hill
until it is no sound at all,
until it comes back over the hill again,
again dragging its furrow,
its ground-rhythm, its wide open throat, behind it.

Cordon Sanitaire

The blanch place, pale, like under a bandage,
a creamy strip of peace
quarantined between cannons like bristles,
like combs' teeth
aligned across from each other. *It's balmy here*
in Cordon Sanitaire, the general wrote
on a postcard, sitting on the veranda
of the Cordon Sanitaire Hotel and Spa. *All's neutral,*
a very light wind-worn tan
the one colour. The back door
of a cannon, the one that swings open
so that a man can insert
a large large shell – Did I,
he thought, did I just hear one
swing open? *I ate the veal*
last night, mashed potatoes, some florets
of cauliflower. He didn't mention,
or else an editor struck it from the text,
the black smoke
flowing from the high stacks on low buildings;
he didn't mention
the little song he sang: 'Leprosaria, Crematoria,
Adiosia, in Memoria.'
His secretary, who was there,
his last unmarried daughter, there also,
said he didn't actually sing
but made its rhythms seem 'liturgical'.
He'd even 'bounce a little' in his chair,
his daughter said,
until the sky turned to lead, she said, until
the sky turned to lead.

The Language Animal

Because he can speak, because he can use his words, a whole headful
of them, he gives everything
names, even things that call themselves,
forever, something else.
Because he can speak he can efficiently lie,
or obscure with such brilliance
a listener with less language
is glad to lose more of it.
Because he can speak
he will be lonely
because those who speak back speak another language
of other derivations.
Because he can speak he speaks.
Because he can speak he can pray out loud.
Because he can speak the predators are drawn to him in the night.
Because he can speak
he invented the ear, then two, to better hear himself speak.
Because he can speak he thought he could sing.
Because he can speak
he has one more thing to do
besides searching for food,
or hiding so as not to be food.
Because he can speak he draws a full breath
and speaks,
in sentences, each one beginning with a large letter
and ending with a period,
or the soon-to-be-invented marks
that indicate bewilderment and awe.

Pencil Box Shaped Like a Gun

You brought to school that fall
the pistol-shaped pencil box, .45-
calibre-inspired but larger, swollen, loaded
with pens, six-inch ruler, the compass tool – the one
with which you got to stab the paper
and make the stubby pencil
strapped to its other leg move around in a perfect circle.
Also an eraser,
like the rubber hammer
the doctor plunked your knee with
once or twice a year. Blue, a see-through
plastic pencil box atop
the scarred (your uncle Larry's name dug deep) desk,
strata after strata of shellac.... The classroom's large
light-filled windows bright,
and Linda Miller's voice
rasps over a speaker, a box with dials, connected
by wire to where she lives,
two or three miles away, over a small river,
halfway up the long grade
of some stubby, stony hills.
Linda's ill, very ill.
We strain to hear
her voice. The teacher talks to the box,
to Linda, whom we hear brokenly
this autumn
of bright skies,
of hay stacked to the rafters,
of swollen pumpkins and gourds,
and of the last cabbages waiting,
any day now, stripped of their
outer leaves, to become part of
a tasty soup.

The Corner of Paris and Porter

Meet me there, you remember, the corner
of Paris and Porter. We stood on that spot
after walking our city all day,
dropped-off-the-earth lost in each other.
We'd live in the house there, we said,
we loved the sway-back porch, the elms
in the yard towering. We stopped
in the thick, still shade of one,
the sidewalk raised and cracked by its roots.
On the curb: a mailbox, agape, flag up,
a dry birdbath in the yard,
and in the driveway a yellow car: this was lucky,
a yellow car, a child once told me.
The sunlight a wall slamming down
outside the shade's circle. Two old sisters, we guessed,
lived there: two
lace antimacassars
on two wicker porch chairs.
We'd knock on the door,
tell them we love their house,
which they'd then bequeath to us,
on the corner, the house
we found by chance, chirps and childcalls,
the clanking of lunch dishes,
though we saw not one child or bird.
The mailman (we never saw him but knew his name
was Steve) would leave great piles
of letters, the grocery
and the garden would provide.
It was the corner
of Paris and Porter,
in that part of the city
where we'd never walked before – it was south
and farther south, past downtown,
beyond the meat district, the fish market,

past the street of clocks, the tripe stalls,
the brick kilns, the casket factories; we turned
east, a few blocks north,
there was nothing but warehouses
and long blocks of lots,
tall fences topped by barbed wire, behind which
what? We walked over a bridge
(the train tracks beneath were thick with weeds)
and there it was: a neighbourhood – houses,
yards, shrubs, we were talking and talking,
I don't know how many miles, lost
in each the other,
and though we did not know where we were,
we knew where we were going: the corner
of Paris and Porter, remember, the day was blue
and clear, I recall the exact path of an ant,
the mica glinting in the kerbstone, a curtain
parting momentarily at your laugh.
I could have drowned in your hair.
Meet me there,
today, don't be late, on the corner
of Paris and Porter.

The Bandage Factory

Our bandage factory's busy: boxcar after boxcar
of gauze-only trains
empty at the east side unloading dock.
The women wash and fold and sterilise.
The men make the big looms boom
in the bandage room.
And the boys and girls (when we're busy
no one goes to school) stack
and sweep and gather scraps
that we ship downstate
to the babies' and children's bandage works.
On the west side loading dock
at five o'clock,
when we've filled a whole train,
we like to stand there
while it pulls away
(some of the children wave)
and watch our bandages go
out into the world
where the wounds reside,
which they were made to dress.

The Cradle Place

(2004)

Morn came and went – and came, and brought no day.

BYRON

I want the old rage, the lash of primordial milk!

THEODORE ROETHKE

Say You're Breathing

just as you do every day, in and out, in and out, and in each
breath: one tick
of a shaving from a bat's eyelash, an invisible sliver
or a body mite
who lived near Caligula's shin, diamond dust (we each inhale a carat
in a lifetime), a speck of scurf
from the Third Dynasty (that of the abundant
imbeciles), one sulfurous grain
from the smoke of a mortar round, a mote of marrow
from a bone poking through a shallow grave,
a whiff from a mummy grinder
caught in a Sahara wind, most of the Sahara itself,
inhaled in Greenland, sweat dried to crystal on your father's lip
and lifted to the sky
before you were born – all, all, a galaxy
of fragments floating
around you every day,
inhaled every day,
happy to rest in your lungs
until they are dust again
and again risen.

Dry Bite

When the krait strikes but does not loose
his venom: dry bite. What makes the snake choose
not to kill you? *Not Please,*
not I didn't mean
to step on you. He may be fresh out: struck
recently something else. But: if he withholds
his poison,
when does he do so and why?
Can he tell you are harmless to him?
He can't swallow you, so why kill you?
There's no use asking the krait: he's deaf.
In that chemical, that split-billionth
of a second, he decides
and the little valve
of his venom sac
stays shut or opens wide.
Dry, oh dry, dry bite – lucky the day
you began to wear
the krait's snake-eyed mark
on your wrist
and you walked down the mountain
into the valley
of that which remains of your life.

Debate Regarding the Permissibility of Eating Mermaids

Cold-water mermaids, and only on Fridays, said Pope Ignace VII.
Sumerian texts suggest consent if human parts
predecease fishy parts,
but cuneiform detailing this
was lost to tomb robbers.
The British Admiralty, sixteenth century, deemed it anthropophagy
and forbade it,
though castaways, after sixty days,
were exempted
upon the depletion of sea biscuits. Taboo! Taboo!, said the South Sea
Islanders, though a man could marry one
if his aquatic skills
impressed her enough. Conversely, a woman, no matter
how well she swam,
could not marry with a merman. Uruguayans, Iowans,
leave no records on the subject.
The Germans find it distasteful,
though recently declassified World War II archives
suggest certain U-boat captains...
No problem for the French: flambéed or beneath béarnaise.
The official Chinese position is they don't have a position!
– But I grow weary of this dour study,
tired of the books
wherein this news is hidden, the creaking shelves
in museum basements, the crumbling pages
of the past and future, I'm tired
of this foggy research
to which I've devoted decades
trying to find the truth in these matters
and what matters in such truth.

Rather

Rather strapped face to face with a corpse, rather an asp
forced down my throat, rather a glass
tube inserted in my urethra
and then member smashed
with a hammer, rather wander the malls of America shopping
for shoes, rather
be lunch, from the ankles down,
for a fish, rather mistake rabbit drops
for capers, or pearls, rather my father's bones crushed to dust
and blown – blinding me – in my eyes,
rather a flash flood of liquid mud,
boulders, branches, drowned dogs, tear through Boys Town
and grind up a thousand orphans, rather
finger puppets
with ice picks
probe me, rather numbness, rather Malaysian tongue worm, rather rue,
rather a starved rat
tied by his tail to my last tooth,
rather memory become mush,
rather no more books be written but on the sole subject of self, rather
a retinal tattoo, rather buckets of bad bacilli and nothing else
to drink, rather the blather
at an English Department meeting, rather
a mountain fall on my head than this,
what I put down here, rather
all of the above than this, this:_____.

The American Fancy Rat and Mouse Association

Rat breeders gather
to primp and parade their best – the chinchilla rat,
silks, the Moluccan cream belly – at this dog show
for mice and rats where, if entered a cat,
there would be no crowning
this year of Rat of the Year, Mouse of the Decade.
The judge cradles a quaking contestant in her palm.
Reputations made or broken, breeding secrets, build
a better cancer rat and your pride can turn to cash, pack
another gram of fat
on the thighs of a mouse
and this news shivers up and down the row
of herpetologists here for the show.
Then, in another, a back row,
sit those whose interests lie in mouse and rat aesthetics
rather than in their behavior
or market potential – Oh the beautiful,
beautiful rats, they sigh, oh the beautiful rats.

To Help the Monkey Cross the River,

which he must
cross, by swimming, for fruits and nuts,
to help him
I sit with my rifle on a platform
high in a tree, same side of the river
as the hungry monkey. How does this assist
him? When he swims for it
I look first upriver: predators move faster with
the current than against it.
If a crocodile is aimed from upriver to eat the monkey
and an anaconda from downriver burns
with the same ambition, I do
the math, algebra, angles, rate-of-monkey,
croc- and snake-speed, and if, *if*
it looks as though the anaconda or the croc
will reach the monkey
before he attains the river's far bank,
I raise my rifle and fire
one, two, three, even four times into the river
just behind the monkey
to hurry him up a little.
Shoot the snake, the crocodile?
They're just doing their jobs,
but the monkey, the monkey
has little hands like a child's,
and the smart ones, in a cage, can be taught to smile.

The Devil's Beef Tub

There are mysteries – why a duck's quack
doesn't echo anywhere
and: Does God exist? – which
will remain always *as* mysteries. So
the same with certain abstracts
aligned with sensory life: the tactile,
for example, of an iron bar
to the forehead. Murder
is abstract, an iron bar to the skull
is not. Oh lost
and from the wind not a single peep of grief!
One day you're walking down the street
and a man with a machete-shaped shard
of glass (its hilt
wrapped in a bloody towel) walks toward you,
purposefully, on a mission.
Do you stop to discuss hermeneutics with him?
Do you engage him in a discussion about Derrida?
Do you worry that Derrida might be the *cause* of his rage?
Every day is like this,
is a metaphor or a simile: like opening a can
of alphabet soup
and seeing nothing but X's, no, look
closer: little noodle
swastikas.

Boatloads of Mummies

embarked from Egypt to New Jersey in 1848.
Boatloads of mummies by sail
sold to a pulp mill
to make into paper.
Which venture (one tries to think
what the investors thought) didn't
work out: the stationery resulting
was gray
and gritty
and held not the black depths of ink.
One wonders where the remaining mummies went.
A few were ground to powder
and put in jars, and then on shelves of remedies,
but all the rest, three or four holdfuls,
where did they go
when the vision of capital failed
(as visions do, more often
than they don't), where did
the remaining mummified go?

The Magma Chamber

Here it boils and begins to build, deep in the core,
what will be lava, molten
rock, in great domed cathedrals of rage underground
eventually expelled – to air,
and land. Sometimes
the magma – feeding up into the spreading rift
to fill the cracks
between the separating plates–heals. Sometimes
it needs a way out
and finds it – bang! – and slow, remorseless rivers
of liquid rock, red rivers
of rock, find their way
to the sea – through houses and horses,
over beet fields and putting greens, over hospitals, eating
through, with fire,
anything that wants to stay in its place
and just go on being. The orb
is hot inside, hurt,
which is bad for those who gauge
and receive its rage.
Nothing can stop it
but the sea
which boils where it enters, nothing
but the sea is vast and deep
and cold enough
to take all this poured fury, nothing
but the sea (if it so pleases)
can make a new island, new mountains,
a new republic of hope.

Guide for the Perpetually Perplexed

Don't hurt your brain on this: if the arrow points left,
it's left you should go. Then
take your first right,
then the next right,
again the next right, then another
right. If you head-on a cement truck,
it is as it should be. Too much
perplexity and soon everyone's head
is a revolving hologram of a question mark!
Instead: if the sign says USE YOUR WORDS,
then use your words,
in this order: subject, verb, object.
Instead: if the sign says SHUT THE FUCK UP,
then you should shut the fuck up.
If it comes over the intercom to get in line,
for gosh sakes, then get in line, your wingbones
to the wall and eyes forward.
Do nothing to further perplex the other perplexed.
We'll let you know when it's single file for lunch,
where it's first your placemats of puzzles
and impossible dots to disconnect
followed by your beans, and your brown meat, gray,
over which you'll pray, oh yes, you'll pray,
if you don't want us to break your neck.

The Year the Locust Hath Eaten

They chewed my lawn down to sand
and then polished
each facet of each sand grain
with their relentless wings and then
were up and off again, a huge ball,
a tornado, a rack-clacking
wind of them.
They ate the sheep of all but their wool.
They ate the trees' leaves, then the twigs, then the branches,
then the trunks,
then sent out sappers
for the roots. They gnawed fence posts
leaving parallel rows
of barbed wire
across bald fields.
They took down the haystacks
and found no needles.
They left the bookmobile
tireless and with but one book uneaten: (insert odious book
of your choice).
They consumed the letters in the attic,
all the letters from sea to land
and land to sea,
all the letters of funeral and woo.
Grandma's wedding dress – leaving a wreck
of pearl buttons – they devoured.
They buzz-cut the attic
and its sawdust sifted down
to the second floor–which was when I fled
and left behind the bitten land and the year
the locust hath eaten.

Burned Forests and Horses' Bones

are all we see when we cross the river
to this land. Two or three days, we guess, since the fire
reached this shore
and went to sleep.
This is where it stopped,
not where it started.
Why didn't it leap this narrow river?
We see but wisps, locally, of smoke.
We can't go back the way we came.
Before we crossed
to this scorched shore, we knew: we can't
go back whence we came.
The trail is charred with drifts of ash,
but passable. We are nine men, three women, seven children,
three mules – two pulling carts; the third, a pack
on its back – one dog, one duck.
We see nothing
but the burned bones
of horses, not for miles, nothing not gray or black.
Because his whiteness (though going
a grimy gray) offends us, we'll eat the duck.
Three more days we travel amid smoldering stumps,
crossing sooty streams, no sounds but the screech
our feet make on the black
and squeaky ground.
At night there is no wood with which to build a cooking fire.
Tomorrow we'll hack up an armoire
and kill and roast the dog.
Not one of the children will cry.
We have three mules yet, two carts.
We have one mission: to arrive
where the fire started
and pass over it to the place before the fire began.

Myope

The boy can't see but what's right in front of him.
Ask him about that clock
across the room, he can't see it, or he don't
care. He makes a picture of a mountain–he's looking
at the mountain! – and it comes out fuzzy
and he puts in cliffs and fizzers
that ain't there. Sit an apple down
on the table and he can draw it in pencil, in color, once so right
I almost took a bite.
And he's got a nose on him like a hound.
His daddy says he can sniff a rat in a freezer.
A set of ears, too: he says he hears
his baby brother crying
and I can get to him
just as he opens his mouth to wail
and in my arms it's right to sleep again.
That comes in handy, sometimes. Sometimes
a baby's got to cry.
The boy's a bit odd.
He likes books a lot.
On a hot summer evening,
I swear, he's reading on the porch
and the turning pages make a breeze.

To Plow and Plant the Seashore

His tractor rattles down the dunes: low tide, it's time to plow
the seashore and then follow
with the finer harrow
blades to comb
this rich earth smoother. The bits of shell and weed
will contribute to the harvest.
He's not been farming long – see: he has all his fingers
to their tips. No, he's not been farming
long. Now his field is ready
and it's time to plant his seeds
in earth through which he pulled his farmer's tools.
This year, it's corn: he loves the little yellow crowns.
Yes, this year it's corn, the farmer thinks,
last year the soybeans didn't take
and the yield was: minus-beans, i.e., the seed beans, too, were gone.
Corn will love this rich and muddy ground
and grow in rows over his long but thin two acres.
That's what they gave the farmer: two acres, a tractor
with its partners,
and that little house
in the blue-green sea grass
above his field. Also four chickens.
They gave him four chickens
and a hammer, and a pitchfork.
This is what they gave him
and he was glad for it, and for his title: farmer.
His fields are tilled.
Someday he'll have a daughter and a son.
By morning, the farmer thinks, the shoots
will be up an inch or two.
The wronged one is always the wrong one.

Goofer-Dust

(dirt stolen from an infant's grave around midnight)

Do not try to take it from my child's grave, nor
from the grave
of my childhood,
nor from any infant's grave I guard – voodoo, juju, boo-hoo rites
calling for it or not! This dust, this dirt, will not
be taken at dawn or noon
or at the dusky time,
and if you approach
this sacred place near midnight,
then I will chop,
one by one, your fingers off
with which you do your harm. Goofer-dust: if you want it,
if you need it, then
erect downwind from a baby's grave
a fine-meshed net
and gather it
one-half grain, a flaky mote, an infinitesimally small fleck
of a flake at a time
and in such a way
it is given to you
by the day, the wind, the world,
it is given to you, thereby
diminishing the need to steal
this dirt displaced by a child
in a child's grave.

The Ice Worm's Life

is sun-avoiding, and by burred flanks
they wriggle through the glacier
which they'll never leave
nor ever meet ice worms of a neighboring glacier.
To them is the unexamined life
worth living? By day
a few yards in/under ice
and then wild nights, wild nights
on the glacier's surface
where to them the wind brings pollen, fern spores,
and the algae
that tint the blue frozen water red. The ice worms gorge,
they gorge, thousands of them,
in the dark, in the cold, aspiring to grow
from one-tenth of an inch
to four-tenths of an inch.
All night, the glacier a lawn
of them bent by the wind, and by dawn
they've gone down into the ice to sleep,
to mate, until it is time
to ascend again: our refrigerative
fellow creatures, our neighbors
on the glacier beside ours
who, if we could invite them into our living rooms,
would decompose
in fifteen minutes (that soon!)
and go wherever their theology tells them they must go.

Hospitality and Revenge

You invite your neighbor over
for a beer and a piece of pie.
He says words inappropriate
about your Xmas bric-à-brac.
You shoot him, three times, in the face.
While you complain to his first son
re high off-white-couch cleaning costs,
he shoots you in the face five times.
At your wake, your first son pumps eight
slugs behind his first son's left ear.
Your wife invites your neighbor's widow for tea.

Breakbone Fever

On the femur a brick drops hard, from the top rib
to bottom a steel
bar slams, on neck bones and skull, on clavicle, the fever
drops its stones, on the knuckles,
the wrist bone; the carpals, both regular and meta-, they get
cellar doors slammed on them. Oh the capitate, hamate,
lunate, and pisiform bones take a bad
beating: ball-peens bang
and jackhammers
jack against each one. Even some joints – interphalangeal
agony! – ligaments, get this fever, go down
with it; even fingernails, nerveless themselves, battered by it,
and hair, hair enters the skull like a hot needle. Watch
out, ossicular chain – hammer, anvil,
stirrup, bones smaller than grains of rice
in the ear's pea-sized cave,
full grown since birth, first to turn
to ash, watch out – the pain there
will tell you who owns the heat,
who aligns the tenses – past, present, future, and none,
will show you who owns the fishhook frictive verbs,
who assigns the persons, places, and things,
who islands the ocean, who affords the tree its rings,
who owns, in fact, your blistering bones.

Monkey Butter

Monkey butter's tasty, tasty,
you put it in cookies and pie,
you mix it in cake, I can't tell you a lie:
don't be light with it, nor hasty
to push it aside. It's not too sweet,
with a light banana-y hue,
the monkeys all love it,
and so will the one you call *you*,
the you who's another you want to love you.
Put it in his pudding, in her pastry puff,
then sweep the table of all that other stuff.
Later, leave a little in his left, her right, shoe.

Can't Sleep the Clowns Will Eat Me

(for Claudia)

it says on the dead
author's ('the author is dead') daughter's
T-shirt. He sympathises with this line
and his daughter who wears it,
and recognises that its author (who also
must be dead) wrote the line to describe
and mock dread, insomnia, fear.
The author, her father (continuing to be dead), buys
the shirt for his above-mentioned child
because she *likes* the line.
The author (dead as a brick) is glad
his daughter enjoys and understands
the line, that it's funny, parodic, odd.
This pleases the author (a rotting corpse)
and – forever, down the boulevard of elms and ash,
forever beside the indeterminate river into the long night,
forever with his child and their blood-on-blood – he will,
he will be happy
learning to live with being dead.

Render, Render

Boil it down: feet, skin, gristle,
bones, vertebrae, heart muscle, boil
it down, skim, and boil
again, dreams, history, add them and boil
again, boil and skim
in closed cauldrons, boil your horse, his hooves,
the runned-over dog you loved, the girl
by the pencil sharpener
who looked at you, looked away,
boil that for hours, render it
down, take more from the top as more settles to the bottom,
the heavier, the denser, throw in ache
and sperm, and a bead
of sweat that slid from your armpit to your waist
as you sat stiff-backed before a test, turn up
the fire, boil and skim, boil
some more, add a fever
and the virus that blinded an eye, now's the time
to add guilt and fear, throw
logs on the fire, coal, gasoline, throw
two goldfish in the pot (their swim bladders
used for 'clearing'), boil and boil, render
it down and distill,
concentrate
that for which there is *no*
other use at all, boil it down, down,
then stir it with rosewater, that
which is now one dense, fatty, scented red essence
which you smear on your lips
and go forth
to plant as many kisses upon the world
as the world can bear!

God Particles

(2008)

Oh, to vex me, contraries meet in one.

JOHN DONNE

I do not remember our friend's name, but he was a good man.

RALPH WALDO EMERSON,
on leaving Henry Wadsworth Longfellow's funeral

Behind the Horseman Sits Black Care,

and behind Black Care sits Slit Throat with a whip,
and on Slit Throat's shoulders, heels in his ribs,
there, there rides Nipple Cancer, and on her back
rides Thumbscrew. No one rides Thumbscrew's shoulders.
Certain suicide, everyone knows not to try that,
everyone, that is, who wants to get older.
Even Pee Stain, the kid whose lunch money,
instead of being stolen,
he's forced to swallow,
even Pee Stain
knows not to ride Thumbscrew's shoulders.
The Horseman (and, presumably,
his horse) prefers none
of this – Black Care with his arms
around his waist as if he's his girlfriend
and those others stacked atop him
like a troupe of acrobats, unbalanced.
The Horseman desires a doorway,
a cave's mouth, a clothesline – or best: a low, hard,
garrotey branch.

The Hungry Gap-Time,

late August, before the harvest, every one of us worn down
by the plow, the hoe, rake,
and worry over rain.
Chicken coop confiscated
by the rats and the raptors
with nary a mouse to hunt. The corn's too green and hard,
and the larder's down
to dried apples
and double-corned cod. We lie on our backs
and stare at the blue;
our work is done, our bellies flat.
The mold on the wheat killed hardly a sheaf.
The lambs fatten on the grass, our pigs we set
to forage on their own – they'll be back
when they whiff the first shucked ears
of corn. Albert's counting
bushels in his head
to see if there's enough to ask Harriet's father
for her hand. Harriet's father
is thinking about Harriet's mother's bread
pudding. The boys and girls
splash in the creek,
which is low but cold. Soon, soon
there will be food
again, and from what our hands have done
we shall live another year here
by the river
in the valley
above the fault line
beneath the mountain.

Hitler's Slippers

were hand embroidered, first with a round, red
rising sun, upon which, centered,
was sewn the symbol – who would bow
for long to such a crippled
wheel? – by which his reign is known.
Hitler's slippers were a gift
(someone else opened the package for him) from a mother,
grandmother, who bent over them for months.
She knew no other way to serve him, therefore, stitch
by stitch she adorned his slippers,
two-thirds of the Axis
represented (*ciao* Italy already)
to please the leader's eyes when he slung
his legs out of bed in the bunker
to begin another day with dry toast,
milk, and one egg, poached.

Sleep's Ambulance

takes me to a quiet room down the long hallway, into the golden elevator,
which *whooshes* me beneath – the wheat fields are stripped
but the hay fields green – down to the many streams, estuaries
like the veins on the back of a hand, flowing to the fingers' tips
and draining into the air beyond.
Did someone turn a soothing siren on?
I think I hear a siren. The factory whistle – Father's home
for supper before the evening shift? It's something of a squeaky song.
Happy little mice, I think, eating through a sack of bones.

Lump of Sugar on an Anthill

The dumb ants hack and gnaw it off grain by grain
and haul it down to the chamber
where they keep such things
to feed their queen and young. The smart ants
dig another entrance, wait for rain.
Which melts the sugar,
and through viaducts they direct it
to their nurseries, the old ants' home, the unantennaed ward,
and so on – the good little engineering ants!
The dumb ants have to eat their sugar dry.
Put your ear to a dumb ant's anthill's hole–mandibles on
sandpaper is what you'll hear.
The dumb ants pray it doesn't rain *before*
they've done their task,
or else they will drown – in sweetness,
but drown, nonetheless.

Stink Eye:

what the mongoose gives the cobra. The eye
that says: be confident
with your poison while
I kill you with my teeth – nonvenomous,
nor as sharp. Stink
Eye: the slit-eyes of a boy
on the trolley from Tijuana
to San Diego, late, telling me: where you get off,
I get off and rob you. Stink Eye: mine,
saying to him, Good luck, *fututor matris*,
which means motherfucker
in Latin. My whole life I've been an educator;
the children come to me
to learn their ABCs.
Stink Eye: the broken, bitter eye
of spite – keep that eye from me, and
furthermore, Lordy, Lordy,
keep me from wearing that eye,
which looks outward and leaks inward,
eating first the brain
on its way to eating the heart.
Only these things: blindfolds, clouds
of cataracts, sharp sticks,
eyewash of acid, lids sewn
shut, lids sewn open
facing nuclear blast, every boy armed
with a BB gun—only these,
and one more hope as recourse
against Stink Eye: hold
the gray backside of a mirror
to your face and return it
to its sender.

The Lead Hour

A block of black salt sits
on his chest and on that
a block, a city block, of ice.
Swallowed: one ton (metric) of metal shavings.
In his pockets: every cannonball on earth
except the ones glued in pyramids
near cannons on town hall lawns.
His wallet's solid steel, size of a toaster!
Like the men pulling the guy wires
on the *Hindenburg* just before the spark
was set: that same strength
hauling his eyelids down.
Two hours before dawn: the lead hour.
Late afternoon, winter: the lead hour.
He's got his stone visor on, stone shoes,
and granite cravat, a bag on his back
full of hammers' heads: ball-peen, claw, and sledge.
Each finger held down by staples
big as goalposts! Notwithstanding,
after all, in any event – under it,
under the lead hour,
he works.

The First Song

was sung after the first stone was thrown at a beast,
after a spear in a man's hand
brought down a pile of meat.
Of course we sang of that!
We hardly had a language and we sang.
We sang the stories, which turned into better stories,
which is why stories are told
and told again. Then, when we had more time
and bellies full enough with food,
we sang of love. But it began
with stones and sharpened sticks,
then sharpened sticks hardened
in fire.

The General Law of Oblivion,

Mr Proust called it: the beloved gone so long
you forget what he/she looks like,
no matter portraits, photos, or memory,
which is the best tool for forgetting.
Though one cannot deny
its genius, Mr Proust's prose
kills me, it loops
me over and out. Is it just French novelists
who don't know how to end
a sentence and so love the semicolon ('the period
that leaks') they can't write two lines
without one? And I am *so* godamned tired
of hearing about that cookie!
As if he were the first (first fish were!) to notice
the powers of the olfactory! But
about the General Law of Oblivion
he had it zeroed: 'It breaks my heart
that I am going to forget you,' he said
in a last letter to a friend.
The length and music of *that* sentence
is perfect, in English or in French.

Midmorning,

accompanied by bees
banging the screen,
blind to it between them
and the blooms
on the sill, I turn pages,
just as desperate as they
to get where I am going.
Earlier, I tried to summon
my nervous friend,
a hummingbird, with sugar
water. The ants got there first.
Now, one shrill bird
makes its noise too often,
too close: *ch-pecha, ch-pecha-pecha.*
If he'd eat the caterpillars
(in sizes S to XXL!) eating my tomatoes,
we could live as neighbors, but
why can't he keep quiet
like the spiders and snakes?
I spoke to an exterminator
once who said he'd poison
birds but he didn't want me
to write about it. I have not
until now, and now starts up
that black genius, the crow,
who is answered by the blue
bully, the ubiquitous, the utterly
American, jay.

The Republic of Anesthesia

I don't feel anything today, my country-
men and -women, I'm numbed by 21 liters
of Novocain, I feel nothing
from my cowlick to the final ridge of my big toe's nail; my tear
ducts dry-walled, not a sob
or the sigh of an ant left in me this autumn,
another autumn
in which the world hates itself so much.
Man ties severed head of another man
to the tail of a dog.
One frog eats a smaller frog.
Wisdom teeth, instead of being yanked,
evolve to wisdom fangs.
All day: arid hairsplitting, cheese-paring.
One bank buys another bank
and the little rubber thimble
on the teller's thumb – that stays the same.
Certainly my god
can rip the heart from your god's chest
and will, god willing, with my help.
A trillion-milligram hammer,
the arc of its swing
wide as a ring
of Saturn, hits us first
on the right temple,
then on the left. *Good night, good night,
lights out!* bark the stars.

Man Pedaling Next to His Bicycle

(for Laure-Anne Bosselaar)

Look at him go
nowhere, his feet whirring, furious. He bends forward to cut
drag, the flair
of his hat shooting the air
over it and down its back slope
for propulsion. Up hills
he's on his toes,
stands and pushes – it's slower
than usual going nowhere next to his sleek, ultralight,
green racer, which is upright,
kickstand unemployed; unridden.
Ring-ring, goes my bell, he says.
Fly in the wind, handlebars' white streamers, he says.
Flapflapflapflapflap goes the ace
of spades in the spokes.
When the road turns downhill he pedals *ahead*
of his bicycle until it catches him,
but never passes him, at the bottom
which opens to the salt flats, the listless,
grayish-white rest of the ride,
the long, level, parching road.
He pedals
beside his bicycle, pedals
and pedals,
wondering where the mountains went,
the pastures, swing sets, the humans tending
to human things. Where did they
go – that which, those whom, he was meant to glide past,
or love, on his journey?

Her Hat, That Party on Her Head

I saw first, and only, her hat. I saw neither face nor shoulder.
No lawn or garden nearby.
No white tablecloths, champagne flutes,
or trays of treats pierced by toothpicks
that fit
with her hat
at this place: a side street in a village in a country
across a border. Looking, with bad directions,
for a bus, brought me here.
Behind a rectory, a priest, in his robe, read
a newspaper, leaning back in a chair
with his bare
feet on a table. I've never seen
such white feet!
I saw also: dust, stained laundry on lines, two roosters.
Some sagging wires hung above.
Then, on the other side of a fence, her hat rising
and dropping with each step.
She walked the fence's length and disappeared.
She returned and walked the fence again.
She was walking a circuit, pain's little looping course.
She walked slowly
and too often her head tipped forward: her eyes turned down
beneath the garden, the birthday party,
on her head. Who is gone so long from her?
Beneath the bougainvillea and lily,
beneath fuchsia's little lamps,
beneath the yellows and greens and blues,
whose absence
made her wear this hat
to help, but fail, to let this absence go?

God Particles

God explodes, supernovas, and down upon the whole planet
a tender rain of Him falls
on every cow, ladle, leaf, human, ax handle, swing set.
We rush from our houses,
farmers standing, saved, in the rain after years of drouth.
Like snowflakes, each God particle is different,
though unlike snowflakes,
are warm and do not melt
but are absorbed by the skin.
Every human, every creature, rock, tomato on earth
is absorbing God!
Who just asked: Why did God explode?
And why ask this far into the story?
I believe He did it to Himself: *nobody*
walks into God's house, His real house, on a hill
in Beulah Land, *nobody*
walks into His house wearing a suicide belt.
No plane flies high enough to drop a bomb on His house.
No one will trespass
to plant an IED in His driveway.
Why did God do it?
Guilt because He sent His son
to do a job He should have done Himself?
I don't think so. God knows,
there's no reason for God to feel guilt.
I think He was downhearted, weary, too weary
to be angry anymore, or vengeful,
or even forgiving, and He wanted each of us,
and all the things we touch
and are touched by,
to have a tiny piece of Him,
though we are unqualified
for even the crumb of a crumb.

Their Feet Shall Slide in Due Time

Hard, balanced in their stance, the truth setting the eye
to the rifle scope's crosshairs, where X,
where all evil, lies.
Steady the hand,
pull back the pointing finger (*squeeeeze*,
don't jerk, the trigger, each century's
manual says). A man's a problem? Kill
the man. Problem's gone. Stalin said something like that,
or was it Gandhi? Deuteronomy
says, in a book of metaphors, sooner
or later the wicked, the venal,
shall face a steep, greasy hill whose fortress
they cannot take. Their feet shall slide
sooner or later: the fall, the reward, uh-huh, the fiery lake,
or the happy place.

Invective

Boils, pocks, and blood blisters, I pray you suffer them,
your goat grow fevered
and leak the yellow milk, I pray moles claw holes
in your head, stones be always in your shoe, fire
in your neck, slop in your cooking pot.
I pray there be rubber bullets in your gun,
I pray your daughter marry for love,
I pray your son wish to be a poet.
I pray your mother take a young lover in front of your father,
I pray it be revealed you keep your toothpicks in your beard,
I pray you be turned down
if you register to vote, I pray your wife fucks you
in the ass, I pray all your lug-nut-dumb offscourings
disdain you, I pray your next breath,
and each one thereafter, fills your lungs
with the stink of your corpse.

Jesus' Baby Teeth

for sale: left front canine (C), two upper
right molars (I, J), and his two front teeth (E, F),
which were all he wanted
for Christmas. Stains,
wear patterns on molars indicate a diet
of fish, coarse bread, and watery wine.
Also for sale: the right forefinger
of Saint Thomas, the one that plugged the hole
in Jesus' side, which action was wasted because
he didn't die (or, he *did* die
but then arose,
which is enough like not dying
to be not dying!) anyway. Also
a swatch of blue from the sleeve
of Mary's robe where you-know-who
laid his downy head. We're also offering
a piece (6″ x 8″) of the True Cross, which is signed
by the other Mary,
the one we love less
for her heart of gold.
Click on thumbnails for pictures of Jesus' left thumbnail, lost in an accident
by hammer, on the job.
Its bright moon is half risen above the horizon
but not one star
in its cracked, blackened sky.

How Difficult

for the quadriplegics to watch
the paraplegics play.
How difficult the day
the ventilator of one lung
shut down, the heart's monitor saying
ta-thump, ta-thump, ta-thump
and the screen showing *aaaaaaaaaaaa*,
and the lady down the hall
howling: *My legs are on fire! My legs are on fire!*
How difficult the icy abstract of the wintry mind.
How difficult *the cracking of houses at their ruin.*
How difficult to mow an empty grave's grass.
How difficult to ride
the landslide's lip descendingly, to endure
the day's chop-logical drip-feed of lies,
how difficult hearing
God's last scratchy – what did He say? – radio broadcast.
What did He say
about no more verbs
in the future tense?

Apology to My Neighbors for Beheading Their Duck

First, it was an accident: I did not mean
to sever his head. A book, or a being superior
or Superior, did not command it thus.
He'd gotten into the little yard we share.
He stood as still as if he were made of cement,
which, in fact, he was. Nevertheless, he was not meant
to lose his head. So that I could lop it off,
a text was not interpreted, though he was
a heterodox duck – he wore a little blue hat.
This color is proscribed for a duck's hat.
Otherwise: white duck, orange feet and beak.
A decent duck, a cause-no-trouble duck.
He weighed a hundred pounds, weighted down
your car to get him here to his new home.
Without his head, he weighs five pounds less.
Without his head, broken at the neck,
he's a less impressive duck,
but still I had no right to take it.
It belonged to him,
and he needed it, his head,
as we, as all creatures, do,
despite the swamp, the sump, thriving inside it.
He did not belong to me,
nor was he of my family.
When I dropped a bag (rather than carry it
down to the barrels beside the duck) of trash
from my fourth-floor back porch,
that's what did it, clipped it clean off,
for which I offer apologies and cash,
but I must reiterate: a book
did not tell me I had the right to do so,
nor did I hear a voice,
a promise, from a pearly place.
I did it dumb and owe you fifty bucks!

The Joy-Bringer

breaks the light through the oak leaves at dawn.
The joy-bringer injects the red bird's red.
The joy-bringer brings the green, lets the cup runneth over
into a saucer, from which you can sip.
Gives fish the river, the river the fish.
If by two inches you avoid a piano
falling on your head
and later at the hospital fall in love with the doctor
who removes a few splinters
of ivory and black piano lacquer
from your left calf: the joy-bringer
arranged that. Also the chilled artesian water
spilling from a pipe only two inches above the ground,
from which you drank on your hands and knees,
on a few boards or branches, you bowed in the muck and drank
that sweet cold reaching-up,
you drank among the skunk cabbage, ferns, a small brook
at your back: again, guess what,
the joy-bringer! In fact, let us praise
the joy-bringer for these seven
things: 1) right lung, 2) left lung, 3) heart, 4) left brain,
5) right brain, 6) tongue, 7) the body to put them in.
Thank you, joy-bringer!
And thanky, thanky too for just-mown hay
cut an inch from its roots
to bleed its perfume into the air!

The Happy Majority

...before I join the great and, I believe, the happy majority.

P.T. BARNUM

Before *I* join the happy majority (though I doubt one member happy
or unhappy) I have some plans: to discover several new species
of beetle; to jump from a 100-foot platform
into a pile – big enough
to break my fall – of multicolored lingerie;
to build a little heater
(*oh not to join the happy ones*
until some tasks are done)
beside each tulip bulb to speed its bloom;
to read 42,007 books (list available
on request); to learn to read and/or write
Chinese, CAT scans, Sanskrit, petroglyphs,
and English; to catch a bigot
(*oh not to join the happy ones*
until some tasks are done)
by the toe; to kiss
the clavicle of (name available
on request); to pay my respects, again,
at the grave of John Keats; to abrogate
my position in God's nihilistic
(*oh not to join the happy ones*
until some tasks are done)
dream; to hold my mother's hand as she leaves this world;
to lay my hand upon my father's heart as he does likewise;
and for my daughter to be glad I was her father as I exit, also
(in a hundred years or so), from the conscious to the un-.

Cliffs Shining with Rain

'Tis double death to drown in ken of shore.

W.S.

Why, in a sea storm, though near shore, on a ship shipping water,
the mast cracked, why don't
sailors happily wreck
on the beach, or even
upon the rocks,
and then swim – or wade – the few yards to shore,
where one cannot drown?
They want to sail home, certainly, not lose their cargo, sail home,
not be marooned.
No shore but their own will do.
So all night they bail by bucket
and pump, all hands, all night,
because they know what I never
will, I who can fear
though not imagine
drowning, I with no cargo
to lose, and who's never sailed under wind
from a wharf where my mother
or wife or child stood. They know, the sailors know,
in a mast-snapping storm, no matter how close to shore, they know
that the waves and splintered timber, thrown
against rocks, or reef, or even beach, drawn back and dashed again,
are a bigger risk
than bailing, bailing, throwing goats, anvils, horses overboard, in order to
stand offshore, a mile or two, safe,
in deep water until,
at dawn, the wind swallows itself
and there they are, the broken cliffs,
shining with rain.

The Shooting Zoo

The giraffe can't stand up anymore: he's still tall
but not tall enough. The silverback is bald,
the zebra's black stripes gray. There's a virus at the zoo: the spring-
bok can't prong,
the alligators wracked by cataracts,
the last lion meowls like an auntie's cat.
The penguins walk as if they have a load in their pants!
The vultures are eating sandwiches and plants!
Something's wrong with all the animals: the pandas obstreperous,
the iguanas demand bananas, the loons
are out of tune.
What to do, what to do? Soon,
whatever it is that's deranging them
will pass through their bars,
across their moats,
and then: our dogs and gold–
fish, the little parakeet
who pecks our lips
so we may say it kisses us, soon
they'll start dropping too.
Next: our children? grandma?
The zookeepers don't know what to do, so
print some permits permitting men
to bring their guns to the shooting zoo.

Mole Emerging from Trench Wall, Verdun, 1916

Doing his job, the mole, disturbed no doubt by the shaking
and noisy dirt, but still digging blind,
goes on with the only life he knows.
He's down there why? Eating worms? Roots?
Having his mole-being, his mole-ness?
So, doing his job, he digs, and emerges,
his head and shoulders, from the rear wall of a trench.
Maybe he was heading for Germany, therefore
it's a French trench. Or,
equally likely, he was heading toward France
and poking through the rear
of a German trench.
Moles live in most dirt in most places.
Some moles have noses shaped like stars.
This one does not.
He's a regular mole, a clock-puncher
mole: wake up, dig, eat, sleep, wake up...
This mole emerges,
blinking. Sergeant Falkenhayn sees him,
or Corporal Chrétien.
The mole sees little
because he does not need to in his dark.
Sergeant Falkenhayn
or Corporal Chrétien, one of them,
pinches the mole's shoulders,
softly, between his thumb
and forefinger,
pulls the whole six inches of him free,
turns him around,
puts him back, nose first, in his tunnel,
and lights a match,
which he then turns to the mole's stubby, muscular tail.

The Grand Climacteric

Stonk, stonk, stonk – mortar rounds slide
down tubes and then fly skyward
until they reach their arcs', their parabolas', peaks
(there, for a second's fraction,
they neither fall nor rise) and hang
there until ... what makes them shatter
to white-hot shrap is: explosives,
love of death (which one cannot love
when dead), or a deep, creaking mineshaft
into which so many blind miners go
to find neither gold nor coal
and never ascend again to the surface. Sorry
to say: *Stonk, stonk, stonk, stonk.*

Sex After Funerals

Hesiod (author of *Works and Days*, a solid
book title) advised against it – counterintuitive, you'd think,
from a poet
second only to Homer, if Homer existed.
(If he didn't, second only to: so what!)
And too, Hesiod spent years in bitter
litigation with his brother
over a barren hill farm and one goat.
This advice from a poet who disliked boats.
This from a poet who couldn't play the harp!
This from a man who worshiped goddesses
but disdained women,
this from a harvester who couldn't keep his scythe sharp,
this from a man
beaten to death with a log
and tossed in the sea,
and whose murderers were ID'ed
(humans refused) by his dog.

Autobiographophobia

I shan't tell you about switching his wooden leg
with her wooden leg, I shan't confess
my lies and the lies against me: when I said I loved X
but really loved Y
and was sleeping with Z
to injure the feelings of X
who was sleeping with Z, Y, and me.
Whether I was there or not
when the sky fell, how I learned
the cure for lesions
of the heart, if it's true
or not that I keep, in a coop
on my roof, the only two extant dodo
birds (plus one dodo egg) – my lips
are sewn shut (might as well be!) with baling wire.
I had many funny uncles.
Not one ever put his hand in my pants.
Never met a dipsomaniac
until I left home
and wandered all those years, in and out, through the lives of others.
My life is one filled with blessings.
And if I've been wronged,
then for each wrong I've been multiblessed.
Which is why
I will not confide
my serial poisoning of parakeets.
It would be fruitless
to ask me regarding my part
in the extinction of sheep.
About my childhood: not a peep.
I sold my grandmother's hearing aid,
not only for cash but also to facilitate
my screaming in her face.
I loved my grandmother,
whose husband I did not know.

Because I'm telling the truth,
there is no shame.
Because I'm telling the truth, and I'm sure
it actually happened
(I was there!), because I'm telling the truth,
it is right that I talk only of myself
and never of you, or you, and you, or you.

Blue Vistas Glued

How well God measures His doses! It was yesterday
the blue vistas were glued to the horizon, it was Tuesday
the pale green grasses rushed to darker green, the rivers rushed
to join another rushing – it was yesterday – river.
There were some
assuagements: the hangmen
who hanged homosexuals no longer hanged
for the same offense; more ears were sharpened,
by fear, but sharpened; there were, oh, a million kisses;
there was the child who grew to be human;
there was febrifuge, sweet febrifuge!
There was, from across the charred field,
the smell of lilacs
brought by a breeze. There were days, years,
when the clock's thinking
did not sound like: *me, me, me, me.*
There were impressive ruins.

Sugar Spoon

Low seven digits (1,000,006, approx.), until it's almost as flimsy as tinfoil,
this spoon,
plunged into the same sugar bowl
every morning, two, three, four times – for three-quarters
of a century, longer?
At night, deep in sweetness, it rests.
And at dawn, when the battered coffee pot begins to rattle,
it's still sunk in the white grains,
while outside, snow
drifts to the eaves almost,
or in summer, the sticky sugar hardens
on it in little arctic ridges. On the handle: my father's thumbprint
exactly on top of his thumbprint, thousands and thousands…
Between each print of his: my mother's. It's going
a bruised green in the recesses
of its engraved (viny trees,
sheep?) handle. It cost
a few pfennig once, with its bowl.
It will serve and serve
until the bottom of its shiny curve
grows so thin
a tiny hole opens
and thenceforth it will leave a dusting of its cargo,
a trail, a grainy Milky Way,
across the maple table
from the bowl to my father's, my mother's, coffee cup.

A Clearing, a Meadow, in Deep Forest

One lies down in the meadow, one hears the insects saw and gnaw
in the grass, and above, one hears
some music from childhood, sees a barn swallow diving.
One has these thoughts,
stricken. Clouds hang above the meadow's – how did
this clearing occur? – ragged
treeline. How did it happen, its edges irregular,
not cut for a field
of even rye or oats? When one first breaks
into it, the clearing,
one thinks: not large enough for a farm,
this fodder couldn't feed four cows.
One walks halfway across
and sits down, stricken. This is the place to rest,
one thinks, in the meadow's middle,
this is the place to stop
and wait for the wind, or a star, or a vole's nose
to point one on one's way.

Child Made of Sand

(2012)

Mundo cosi, cosi.
(Such, such is the world.)
ANTONIO DE SOSA,
Diálogo de los Morabutos

Write! Comrade, Write!
EMILY DICKINSON

Joy, shipmate, joy!
WALT WHITMAN

The Moths Who Come in the Night to Drink Our Tears

always leave quenched,
though they're drinking,
in composition, seawater,
which does not make them insane
as it does parched humans when we
drink it, even
with our big, big bodies.
If you knew
a leper's tears do not contain
the bacillus *leprae*,
would you let him weep on your chest?
Let the moths come, let the sandwoman and -man come,
let Morpheus and Dreamadum come
unto me, and my beloveds,
let the moths come
and drink of the disburdening waters.

You and Your Ilk

I have thought much upon
who might be my ilk,
and that I am ilk myself if I have ilk.
Is one of my ilk, or me, the barber
who cuts the hair of the blind?
And the man crushed by cruelties
for which we can't imagine sorrow,
who would be his ilk?
And whose ilk was it
standing around, hands in pockets, May 1933,
when 2,242 tons of books were burned?
So, what makes my ilkness *my*
ilkness? No answers, none obtainable.
To be one of the ilks, that's all
I hoped for; to say hello to the mailman,
nod to my neighbors, watch
my children chmb the stairs of a big yellow bus
that takes them to a place
where they learn to read
and write and eat their lunches
from puzzle trays – all around them, amid
the clatter and din,
amid bananas, bread, and milk,
all around them: them and *their* ilk.

Nietzsche Throws His Arms Around the Neck of a Dray Horse

and it signals the beginning of his final breakdown?
An act of empathy – as if he felt how broken
that broken horse was? He could. Or
was it tertiary syphilis? Unlike
many philosophers – rigid,
tortured by the abstract – it was the concretions
that broke Nietzsche. Were the electric drills
of his migraines physiological,
or did he think too hard
and know not, well enough, how to be loved, or to love,
like most of me?

A Frozen Ball of Rattlesnakes

How'd they get in a ball?
What do you mean by a ball, how many in it,
and do you mean stone-frozen?
Or do you mean dormant, sluggish, half hibernating?
Snakes can do that, right?
Rattlesnakes live in other countries too.
There are many species, right?
I'd seen copperheads and cottonmouths
in some mountains
and a few desultory streams I knew.
I live in a large southern metropolis now
and my neighbors
found a rattler (albeit a small one) in their cellar.
Killed it with a shovel.
They have a child, and a dog.
In the frozen ball, do they wake up one by one?
Are those closest to the middle
warmer than the others?
They're all cold-blooded.
Lincoln used the phrase, metaphorically, more than once.
It's a good metaphor, easy to read, vivid. Metaphors
should be, and sometimes
should terrify: A man chops
off another man's head, props
the corpse sitting up against a roadside pole
and places the man's head in his hands,
on his lap.

The Queen of Truth

If torture is the Queen of Truth
then what is the King of Truth?
Could it be the Black Dog, ennui,
accidie? Can the King
rule by the weight
of the ink (oh, I pray
not the pixels!) on an execution order?
Could the King be numbed by dumdum fever?
Could the King be a thug, theocratic or not?
Might the King's epiphanies be arsenic-lit?
Can the King pass his edicts
from behind a screen?
Maybe not so Long Live the King!
What kind of King passes the torture off
on his wife? Please. Please, Your Majesty,
step up, show us you've got something new!
Something well past torture.
Something long, and slow, and cruel.
The King, outranking the Queen,
who resorts to torture *alone*
to obtain the truths she needs, the King
with his funny hat and ruffled collar,
what can the King do
(let's find out)
that hasn't already been done by the Queen?

A Delivery of Dung

interrupted Wordsworth as he drafted 'Intimations of Immortality'.
A timely wagonload
if one considers only
the title. An honest man knows
there is no such thing – immortality – hints or no hints.
I prefer Wordsworth the Younger,
his early/mid-thirties, when the above mentioned
was written, when he and Dorothy
still had most of their teeth
and before he was spoiled (milk-sopped,
and walking like an alderman
fed on too much turtle soup) by Dorothy (sister),
Mary (wife), and Sara (sister-in-law), and sometimes even another
Sarah (Coleridge's wife, estranged).
Wordsworth the Elder
obtained a sinecure selling stamps,
wrote many bad poems,
lived a long, honorable life, and,
truth is, he is immortal,
or as close as a corpse can get, would be
immortal for the first four stanzas of 'Intimations'
alone. *Those stanzas alone.*
Anonymous – 'Western Wind' – achieved the same with four lines!
No piece of art is perfect.
All it has to do is stay around
for two hundred, or five hundred,
or a few thousand
years. It (art) always changing, us;
not so much.

Elegy

César Vallejo, Arago Clinic, Paris, Holy Friday, April 15, 1938

It was you, César, they killed to the base of your forefinger, you.
Certainly they shot Pedro Rojas too.
No doubt Juana Vásquez was killed.
The killers, poor also, were skilled.
And Emilio, they shot him in the back of the neck
after they made him kneel amid the wreck
of his grandmother's house – they beat
but did not kill her. The people, their hands and feet
(*A cripple sleeps with his foot on his shoulder.*
Shall I later talk about Picasso, of all people?),
these are the people you wrote for, César,
though your later poems, no longer lighted by the laser
of your homeland, of *Heraldos Negros* or *Trilce*,
were real enough for exile but not as true, licit.
Socialist realism, the aesthetic was called,
poetry force-marched – to diminish, equally, all.
It was not right for your mind and betrayed your heart.
Your countrymen and -women should bring you home, César.
Entombed in France is good enough for some,
but Peru should bring Peru's great poet home.

Every Time Someone Masturbates God Kills a Kitten

Why not kill a rat? There're lots of rats! Remember
the time You gave some of them fleas,
which killed them (that was good), but then the fleas jumped off
the dead rats
and bit humans,
who died too, about a third of them
on the planet? You *were*
good to Poland (hardly any occurrences), which You
made up for in following centuries.
How about snakes? Why such vituperation?
Little whips, You made, with such racking poison!
How about clams? Would one clam feel the loss
of another clam in, at least, a version of grief ? I'm not sorry,
I prefer clams to rats or snakes.
I eat clams, but I'm willing to never
eat a clam again – for the kittens.
How about You,
how about adjusting Your plan
a little, how about a little less hard-ass?
How about You tell Your flock it's time to let this bill pass?

West Shining Tree

West, but west of where?
How far west? Northwest, southwest?
I need to get there, un-iambically.
Please send coordinates.
Longitude and latitude, please.
Why is it shining? That affirms light, life,
though west also associates with death,
which also affirms life – if you're not dead.
What kind of tree is it? Leafy? Tall?
Hardwood, fever tree, balsa?
A tree of luminous fruit?
In prose, it's evening light through a tree,
looking east to west.
May it be more: an emblem,
a synthesis of something beyond
another sundown on the back lawn
under the retractable awning.
I want to stand beneath this tree.
I want to put my hand to its bark.
I'll leave tonight, no, Tuesday.
I'll head dead west and ask of all I see:
Which is the way, the long or the short way,
to the west shining tree?

Rue de la Vieille Lanterne

Gerard de Nerval (1808-1855)

Where are the shoelaces of yesteryear, Gérard?
Those with which you hanged yourself
from a streetlamp? Or, as some accounts say,
from a window grating, on this little rathole
street in Paris, where there's a plaque for you.
Perhaps 'window grating' is less poetic in French.
Some called you an early, though not the last, *poète-maudit*.
A poet who walked a pet lobster on a blue leash
seems, however, hardly glum!
Some kind of hide, I'm assuming shoelaces
in the nineteenth century were stout
and long enough to wrap around
your neck a few times.
An early walker of a French dog,
is that who first discovered you, Gérard,
or the last drunk stumbling home?
The shoelaces of yesteryear, where did they go?
The same place as François Villon's snows
of yesteryear, nearly four centuries before you took exit,
the same place as the snows of last winter, and all the winters
in between, and all snows to come.

Like Tiny Baby Jesus, in Velour Pants, Sliding Down Your Throat (A Belgian Euphemism)

– Jenny

It tasted so good; the touch of it tasted so... God,
handless, must have had a hand in it; it wasn't 'like' anything,
though language without simile is like a lung
without air, or air and nary
a lung to breathe. It was like the lip
of a small waterfall, its perfect curve,
the half-breath-held-split-moment
the last few inches of horizontal river
turn into the first few inches of vertical river.
It was like that, or, it was like, but better than,
the word 'negligee' or the word 'nugatory'
or 'lagniappe' (pronounced *lan-yap*: a small gift or tip).
It was, too, like the color of the crow's wing,
in which blue and green burn beneath the black.
I'd compare it to a perfect parabola,
at the exact peak of which
a man shot out of a cannon exclaims: Yes!
I'll land dead center of the net,
let's move the cannon back
twenty feet, increase the powder load, redo the physics,
let's try it again *right now!*
It felt like holding an otter intent
on play, it was like a ptarmigan
on the tundra guarding her eggs,
it was like the moon in the glass eye
of a man lying in the grass
but not like the moon in his good
eye – that's a little puff of cataract.
No, it was not like, nor unlike, anything.
It was her heart carving
the air as she spoke.

Not the Same Kind of Mud as in 'Two Tramps in Mud Time'

The dust motes of mud at a pond's bottom,
sluggish river, or swamp. The finest, most ethereal
of muds, rising in soft pinheads
from the density below; the fog of mud, what first
grips your ankle so whisperly, a little warmer
than the water above it, a satiny sock
saying, *Dip your foot a little deeper into...*
The mud of blur and smudge.
The almost drinkable mud.
The dusk of mud, the passage, the membrane,
the place between less creamy mud
and harder mud, riverbed.
Drifty elixir, reenvisioning
us, red-carpeting us, down.

Why

It is an execrable and damnable monosyllable, why; it exasperates God, ruins us.

JOHN DONNE, Sermon CXXX

Why so much bread rotting on shelves and the mice so fat they roll
to their holes
at night, their legs too short
to pass their bellies to the floor, whyzat?
What starts up the diphtherial winds, melanoma sunsets?
I was also wondering (*So he stood in his shoes /*
And he wonder'd. / He stood in his shoes / And he wonder'd.) why
the years come to resemble a greasy deck of cards,
why afternoons bleed,
why does my friend die
before I've met her in the flesh
which she ordered turned to ash
the minute she was dead?
Now that I'm asking: Why the incapables, thirsty
at the lip only, why
the incapables commanding the capables,
and howzit the broken, melon-kneed horse
is made to kneel
before the bullet to his brain?
I'm full of whys!
Why is there no limit to recrudescence?
Why did that man jump so high
he forgot to come down, why, in a place with no more air,
it still *looks* as if air remains,
why-o, why-o, why?

The Riverine Farmers

Farming by a river, your fields
within twenty feet of its banks' shade trees.
Drinking from the river,
bathing in it, feeding your fields with its waters,
taking fish and, in winter, eels
from beneath the ice
at its crenelated edges,
thanking it for the silt it leaves after spring's snowmelt,
sitting by it in August when it's lowest,
its bigger bed-stones exposed....
What we'd do, because there was a bow
in the river, what we'd do – my brothers
and I – was launch some boats of sticks
and leaves and race across the bow's neck
to see which ones made it
around the bend's swirling eddies,
then watch them ride the little rapids
that slid under the barbwire fence line
ending our land. The boys
sometimes threw stones at the boats,
making boy-noise explosions.
Father stood at the river's edge,
one hand in his pocket,
the other leaning on the walking stick
he needed. On the wind,
a quarter mile upriver, Mother was weeping.
Every year the river. Every year the weeping.
Every year the sowing,
most years the reaping.

Bricks Sinking in Deep Water

At what depth does their dull orange disappear?
I rowed out to where I know the water's deep,
and in my rowboat a cargo
of bricks, fifty balanced
across the stem, just so.
At the bottom of this reservoir
was a town. Two towns, in truth.
Its people were paid an honest price
to leave, but no question: they had to move.
I anchor my boat forty feet above
what was once a pasture.
I take a brick from port first
and hold it by its upper right corner
and dip its lower left corner into the water
before I let it slip my fingers.
The next one I take from starboard,
but drop from port, and so forth and on.
It's the *sinestre* hand that does the work.
I never counted two seconds before one was gone
from touch, and sound, and sight. They sink until they stop
on now drowned and grassless land.
Why do I want to leave a small scattering
of man-made triangular stones
at the bottom of this no-bones
(the cemetery relocated)
body of water? In darkness, who does not love
the faint, hard, orange glow
of building bricks?

Dead Horse

At the fence line, I was about to call him in when,
at two-thirds profile, head low
and away from me, he fell first
to his right front knee
and then the left, and he was down,
dead before he hit the...
My father saw him drop, too,
and a neighbor, who walked over.
He was a good horse, old,
spavined, eating grass during the day
and his oats and hay
at night. He didn't mind, or try to boss, the cows
with which he shared these acres.
My father said: Happens. Our neighbor,
named Malcolm, walked back to his place
and was soon grinding toward us
with his tractor's newbackhoe,
of which he was proud
but so far used only to dig two sump holes.
It was the knacker who'd haul away a cow.
A horse, a good horse, you buried
where he, or she, fell. Malcolm
cut a trench beside the horse
and we pushed him in.
I'd already said goodbye
before I tried to close his eyes.
Our neighbor returned the dirt
from where it came. In it: stones,
stones never seen before
by a human's, nor even a worm's, eye.
With the back of a shovel
we tamped the dirt down.
One dumb cow
stood by. It was a Friday.

For supper we ate hot dogs, with beans
on buttered white bread. Every Friday,
hot dogs and beans.

Outline for My Memoir

The time my horse got stuck in the mud.
(Two paragraphs; no, one.)
Went blind in right eye, took some medicine;
I could see again. Scary detail: when the doctor
first shined the little light
into my pupil, he drew back, startled.
(Three paragraphs.) Later, high school: broken heart.
(Since this happens rarely, milk for three, four
paragraphs.) *Milk*, speaking
of which: I helped my father peddle it,
in a square white truck in a small round town.
College, my twenties: I recall little to interest you.
I did cover many pages with writing,
and read, and turned a thousand
pages for every one on which I wrote.
(Don't see how I can say what else happened then
and be honest.) My thirties? Wore funny glasses.
(Maybe a two-sentence self-deprecatory joke?)
My forties, fifties? The best part
was a child, named Claudia. I could say some funny
things about her, but so could every father.
Besides, family is personal, private, *blood*.
(With above exception of daughter, those two decades:
a paragraph, maybe two if I insert
journal entry on day of her birth?)
I can't bear to write of her mother, whom I hurt.
Lately? Read like a hungry machine,
in a new room, in a house I love; there is still
my child to love, and friends,
and a beloved, named Jenny.
My vital signs are vital.
I tend a little garden, have a job.
(No way I could write more than a few sentences
on these years

under the sentence, again,
of happiness.) If I live a hundred lives,
then I'll know more truths, maybe, and lies,
to write *my* memoir, novella-sized.

INDEX